MORE PRAISE FOR JEFF RAZ AND HIS FIRST BOOK
The Secret Life of Clowns

"If you're curious about the clowning profession, you'll turn these pages."
Bill Irwin, Sesame Street's Mr. Noodle, MacArthur "Genius," and Tony Award winner

"For me, Raz's book is…a tonic. For me, it's about the learning and life-long re-learning of the craft of the performer…I will place it on the shelf beside my other cherished book about my craft, Yoshi Oida's *The Invisible Actor*."
Laurie McCants, *American Theatre Magazine*

"Over the course of the nearly twenty years that I have been publishing *Spectacle* I have been sent several books on clowning…I was able to actually finish reading very few of them. Now along comes a new book by Jeff Raz…His book is one of those tomes on clowning that I raced through with relish, intrigued and fascinated by his story and his down to earth approach to clowning."
Ernest Albrecht, *Spectacle Magazine*

"If this were a juggling routine, I could confidently say "No Drops." (*The Secret Life of Clowns*) should be required reading for clown teachers and for aspiring clowns."
Adam Gertsacov, clownlink.com

"I knew from having lived with a clown for the past decade that clowning crosses over from the stage into reality…What I didn't realize, until reading this book, is to what extent clowning lessons are life lessons."

Samantha Cosentino Baker, CircusTalk.com

"Raz captured two key, but often neglected features of the clown, wandering and being contrary. He ventured to Alaska, Nebraska — now I ask ya, *what* was he thinking? What a clown thinks: where next? And *how* was he thinking? As a clown thinks: what's backwards, unexpected, upside-down? The clown sees the world differently than others, helping re-create a new world."

David Carlyon, Director, actor, ex-Ringling/Barnum clown, award-winning author of *Dan Rice: The Most Famous Man You've Never Heard Of* and *The Education of a Circus Clown*

THE SNOW CLOWN

CARTWHEELS ON
BORDERS FROM ALASKA
TO NEBRASKA

BY JEFF RAZ

The Snow Clown: Cartwheels on Borders from Alaska to Nebraska

For information, contact Jeff Raz at *jeffraz@aol.com*

The Snow Clown and Jeff's first book *The Secret Life of Clowns* can be
purchased at *www.thesnowclown.com* or *www.secretlifeofclowns.com*.

First Edition

Designed by Tracy Cox/Codex
www.itscodex.com

ISBN 978-0-9979048-2-6

In memory of my mother, Mickey Spencer — artist, activist, sociologist, writer, publisher

INTRODUCTION

THIS IS AN ADVENTURE BOOK — *Around the World in 80 Days* with fewer hot air balloons and more bush planes. It is also a story about taking art, specifically circus and theater, out of its comfy confines and into the wild world. The title character uses circus and theater the way the late Anthony Bourdain used food and cooking — as tickets to explore different cultures.

The characters in this book are all fictitious; the action is inspired by my trips to Alaska and Nebraska from the late '70s to the late '90s. People who know me might guess that the work-related details have their roots in historical fact while the sexier parts of the narrator's personal life are pure imagination. They might be right.

If you survive the weather in the first Alaska section, you'll find a few monologues from *Father-Land,* a play I wrote with Jael Weisman that premiered in 1992. I also used two plays written with students at the University of Nebraska, Lincoln — *Noah's Floating House Party* and *All Tangled Up* — as the raw material for a couple of chapters. Shakespeare, Lucille Ball, a Yup'ik ghost and the trickster Raven also make appearances.

Jeff Raz
Alameda California

ACT I

NORTH TO ALASKA

Yukon/Kuskokwim Delta
Winter 1980

CHAPTER ONE

THE FROZEN RIVER
Kwethluk

"TAKE IT, CLOWN BOY. You can fly this crate until we get to the Kuskokwim." The bush pilot lets go of her steering wheel, or what would be a steering wheel if we were in a car. I grab mine, pulling back a little too hard, and the Cessna swoops up sharply. "Easy, Clown Boy. Just keep us here at 500 feet and follow the shoreline."

The Bering Sea, frozen thick, is almost indistinguishable from the tundra. Only ripples in the ice, solid waves, give me a hint of where the shoreline will be in the spring, after breakup. It's February, the dead of winter, the only time the Alaska Arts Council brings performers up from the lower forty-eight. It's the time of year when everyone is grouchy, bored with sub-zero weather and frozen salmon dinners and ready for a couple of clowns to fly in with 21 bags full of juggling balls, costumes, stilts, face-paint, a unicycle and peacock feathers for balancing. Our job is to bring some circus light and warmth to the frozen tundra.

We're just starting our third week, out of seven, flying bush charters and mail planes in and out of Bethel, a town of 4,000 and Southwest Alaska's biggest city. This is my first trip to Alaska in winter and my first long tour ever. It's also my best-paying gig to date and a résumé item that I hope gets me into Dell'Arte International, a big-time theater school.

I grip the handles, trying to keep the plane above the last line of frozen waves, peeking at the instruments every few seconds. Jenny, the pilot, leans back, folds her arms behind her head and closes her eyes. I grip a little tighter. Jenny looks like Xena: Warrior Princess and talks like

Dolly Parton. She's our regular pilot and has been teaching me how to fly a plane since we started this tour, but I thought she was just filling the time and maybe flirting a little. Now she's napping and I'm in control of a Cessna going 150 miles an hour over a frozen wasteland.

The vibrations of the plane and the monochromatic view are starting to un-jangle my nerves. Tina, my clown partner, who always gets the back seat because my 230 pounds are needed up front to counterbalance the luggage, gestures to Jenny. I give a thumbs-up and tip the wings from side to side to show Tina I'm good to go. Without opening her eyes, Jenny smacks me on the top of the head. "Don't get fancy, Clown Boy. I've already had my crash for the year."

Tina yells over the roar of the motor, "What crash?" Jenny, arms still behind her head, tells us about her accident:

"Right before Christmas, middle of the tundra, nasty weather, didn't have the tools to fix the Cessna. Pitched the tent off a wing, good sleeping bag, pretty comfy. I could'a radioed in, I guess, but I figured then I'd have to go down to Nashville for Christmas. Ever been to Nashville?"

She doesn't wait for an answer.

"Don't. Or at least don't visit my family if you do. So, I have my tent and a gun and a little cook stove. Shot some ptarmigan, cooked 'em up nice; already had salmon strips, candy bars and stuff. And a good book. Ever read John McPhee, *Coming into the Country*? Good read, real good. One part, this guy stops a charging grizzly by saying 'shoo.' Just 'shoo.'"

Tina, who is no fan of bears or bush planes, asks, "How long were you stranded?"

"Got back for New Year's Eve. Big party in Bethel. Dry, of course. Didn't want to miss that."

Jenny laughs so hard the plane jiggles. Alcohol is banned in villages on the Yukon/Kuskokwim Delta, which means that "Friday beer" is a favorite drink — "Make it Monday; drink it Friday." Some pilots smuggle in the real stuff from Anchorage, Fairbanks or even Seattle.

Tina says, "Let's not crash today, OK? I'm not fond of ptarmigan — I'm a fried chicken kind of gal." Jenny laughs again, "Hey, Clown Boy's doin' good," but she takes the controls and I exhale.

A few minutes later, Jenny points across my body, "There's the Kuskokwim. We'll land on the river when we get to Kwethluk; they haven't plowed their landing strip for weeks." The Kuskokwim River looks like an unmarked white highway heading east from the Bering Sea. Soon we see a small cluster of houses sitting on the edge of the frozen river and Jenny starts easing the Cessna down.

We skid to a stop and the propeller slows enough to see the individual blades. I unbuckle and Jenny says, "Don't step out 'til I tether the prop. Had a guy once, got out too early on a river like this. Ice was slick and the wind was up. Slid right into the blades. Hamburger. Ugly." I sit very still until Jenny gives a thumbs-up through the windshield.

Tina and I pull on our coats, hats and mittens, step out on the ice and start to unload. We've gotten used to 20 below, sort of.

The last two pieces to come out of the plane are bundles of brightly painted wooden stilts, seven feet long two-by-twos with triangular platforms for the kids' feet. They are tied together with their ends wrapped in burlap. As we lean the stilts on our pile of duffels, heavy-duty garment bags, suitcases and canvas sacks, Jenny waves, jumps in the plane and starts the prop. A few moments later she's a spot in the distance.

CHAPTER TWO

COMING INTO THE COUNTRY
Kwethluk

IT'S QUIET. TINA AND I STAND on the frozen river looking out at a world of white. We're alone. The sun is starting its long slide down along the horizon. School will be out soon. Did anyone hear our plane land? Are they coming to pick us up? The wind cuts through our jackets. I pull my hood up and make a tunnel for my face with the fur. We wait.

Tina booked this tundra tour through Stephanie Jennings, an Arts Council representative we met at the Alaska State Fair last fall. Tina and I were performing with the Bay City Reds, a hot "new vaudeville" quartet out of San Francisco. I joined The Reds a little over a year ago and it was my first full-time professional gig — I'd performed on the streets, at Renaissance Faires and in small circuses since I was 15, but this was a big step up.

Our act started with a trio of jugglers, one of them me, in red striped shirts and black capri pants throwing nine clubs. Then a dowdy lady walks out of the audience and right through the flying clubs (Tina in a wig and frumpy coat). The audience is fooled, at least for a moment. After a slew of near misses and genuinely funny patter, the three jugglers rip away Tina's coat to reveal, ta da!, her own red striped/black capri costume. The formerly frumpy lady picks up three clubs, the quartet does some nifty twelve-club patterns, then a big bow followed by a lot of offers to work hotel events, corporate parties and state fairs.

I loved being a pro and, despite my iconoclast Berkeley Boy image, I liked being part of a company with business meetings and strict schedules and well-structured rehearsals. I loved the sound of the clubs clicking into our palms in perfect rhythm then the split second of silence between the last catch and the applause. And I loved being successful at something, finally finding a profession that got me out of my big brother's shadow.

When I was little, before my dad died — he'd been a photographer in the war, became a physicist and ended up bipolar — we lived on Long Island. My brother was a year ahead of me in school and I always got his old teachers. Every year my teacher would say, "Oh, you're Alan's brother! I'm so glad to have you in my class." And every year, after a month or so, my mother would get called in for a conference. One teacher even told her, "Not every child can be as brilliant as Alan. Mental retardation is nothing to be ashamed about."

Luckily, my mother is fierce, smart and tenacious. She fought the schools for me and tried to fight my growing insecurity. She once got my brother and me IQ tests and then told us that our scores were identical. She's never wavered from that story and I still half believe her. And she's always supported my performing, although she didn't like it that I had to travel with the Bay City Reds. Last fall, when I told her that I was flying up to Alaska to perform at the state fair, she said, "You're the biggest damn Jew on any plane — keep your mouth shut or the hijackers will kill you first."

A gust of wind blows my hood back so I turn to face the other way. Looking down the Kuskukwim, past the pile of gear, there is nothing to distinguish river from land. There is nothing but snow.

The Alaska State Fair is an hour outside of Anchorage and a world away from this frozen tundra: long sunny days and short nights lit by curtains of aurora borealis; mountainsides red with fireweed; rodeo rings full of dust, bulls and even a Tibetan yak; bluegrass pickers with monster chops honed in warm kitchens during the nine-month winter; and huge Bisquick pancakes full of fresh-picked mountain blueberries. Stephanie Jennings runs the pancake booth at the Fair in summer; the rest of the year she is the Arts Council representative in Bethel. At the Fair, Tina got pancakes for breakfast every day, stayed to chat, and, on the last day, Stephanie offered her this tundra tour. "All you need to do is find a partner, preferably male, to balance the ticket."

Tina asked me to go with her, told me how much Stephanie was paying and I jumped at it. I was already in love with Alaska (and a little in love with Tina), the other Bay City Reds were talking about disbanding the act and I needed money to go to theater school. Circus stuff is fine but I want to use my mind as well as my body. I want to make shows with ideas and words and politics and emotions. Maybe do a solo play using stories about my crazy family. I want to be able to make people cry as well as laugh. But to do *anything* beyond circus, I need theater school — and for theater school, I need money and experience. Alaska was a gold mine for prospectors; now it's going to be a gold mine for a clown who would be an *artiste*.

"It's too cold to just stand here waiting. Let's go." Tina starts walking toward the village and I follow, leaving our little hill of circus props to slowly turn white with blown snow. We see the lights in the biggest building in Kwethluk and know it must be the school. It's quiet as we walk on the frozen river, picking our way in the half-light.

After a few minutes we hear a hum. A black shape is coming toward us across the white snow. It gets bigger and louder. A snowmobile pulling an empty sled stops next to us and a teenager in tan insulated coveralls says, "Want a ride?" His vowels are flat and slide out from behind his front teeth, a village accent. Tina pulls down the scarf she's got across her mouth and says, "Can you get our stuff? We'll walk." The boy gives a little wave and roars off, the snowmobile's front skis sliding over the ice. We walk on, huddled in our down jackets.

Before leaving San Francisco, Tina and I carefully went through the list of winter clothes the Arts Council sent us: Sorel boots with leather uppers, rubber soles and thick felt liners; long underwear; warm scarves; and the best hooded down parkas, rated to keep you warm to 40 degrees below zero Fahrenheit — Tina's is red, mine is dark green. I decided to make my own mittens: handmade leather shells trimmed at the wrist with rabbit fur and decorated with Tlingit designs with store-bought wool mittens inside.

A few minutes after we stepped off the plane in Bethel, I knew I'd have to make some wardrobe adjustments: the mittens were too tight (an air pocket is the key to warmth in the Arctic), the Tlingit designs came from a culture 1,000 miles southeast of the Yukon/Kuskokwim Delta and my hood didn't have a ruff. My Jewish nose froze.

So Stephanie took me shopping, first for huge army surplus mittens and then three kinds of fur to make a ruff — rabbit close to the skin for comfort, otter next since it's waterproof, and wolf on the outside to trap body heat. We went to a Yup'ik fur trader's house to pick out the skins, which were already cut in strips for ruffs. I chose a wolf strip with the tail on it — the idea of roaming the Arctic with a wolf tail wagging behind my head seemed dashing and artistic. Stephanie made sure I got a written note, with the trader's signature, so that I could legally own the wolf pelt. The last stop was the general store for a small piece of brown corduroy for backing and waxed dental floss to use as thread.

Back at Stephanie's house, a converted hotel on Bethel's main drag with topographically challenging floors, I borrowed a glover's needle to sew the ruff. When I finished, I used some leftover rabbit fur to make a little nose guard with a strip of elastic to hold it in place; a brown-and-white fur clown nose.

We hear the hum of the snowmobile behind us as we're walking up the slope from the riverbed to the school. A moment later the sled, piled high with our equipment, whizzes by and a red plastic tackle box bounces off. It flies open and little round tins of black, white and red makeup scatter in the snow. Tina picks up the case; I brush off the tins and put them back in.

We find our way into the overheated front hall of the school, stomping the snow off our Sorels and shedding clothes before we sweat too much. The kids come from everywhere, hugging our legs and opening our bags, which they had dragged in from the sled a few minutes ago. They are laughing and throwing juggling balls and asking questions.

This is our third village, the third time we've been swamped by Eskimo kids. I realize again how uncomfortable I get the moment a dozen strange children climb all over me. Tina is fine, asking for names and letting them feel her wavy red hair. The little ones all have heads of thick, straight black hair that hold a faint smell of seal oil, a staple out here. A few of the teens and tweens have curled their hair with Toni home perm; red hair is new and novel. After freeing myself from the mob, I pick up two of the duffels and start to schlep them down the hall to the gym.

The kids see me and Tina's hair is forgotten, the balls are back in the bag, there's some pushing and shoving and then, without a word, they are behind me carrying all of our stuff. A couple of teenagers take the duffels out of my hands. We are guests and guests are special here.

The gym is brightly lit with halogen lights. The hardwood floor gleams, the basketball nets are bright white and there are two piles of blue wrestling mats in the corner. These kids go to a modern, well equipped school a short walk from their homes. Their parents and grandparents were sent away to Indian high schools in Oklahoma, breaking up families and crippling the Yup'ik language. In 1973, a girl named Molly Hootch sued the state to force them to provide a high school in her village. She won and now every village, even this tiny one, has a school. Every school is the center of the village and the basketball court is the center of every school.

A small, smiling man in his forties with military-cut brown hair comes into the gym. His insulated coveralls are unzipped to the waist and he's slipped out of the top part, letting the outfit's arms and torso bounce behind him like a hollow, headless twin.

"You must be the circus program. Welcome to Kwethluk. I see Eddie got your stuff. Good, good. I'm Kyle Stern, the principal here." He has a pinched nasal drawl from somewhere deep in Dixie. We introduce ourselves, shaking hands with a firm grip and one sharp downward pump, the village style. Kyle gets the kids to put our stuff in a closet and apologizes for our sleeping quarters, which are right next to the closet and not much bigger.

"At least you'll keep each other warm — body heat in a small space, that's Eskimo central heating." He winks at me then leers at Tina, who stares him down. "Anyway, school starts at 8:00 but the kids usually play basketball before class. It'll get loud in here by 7:30 so you might want to be out of your PJs by then. Anyway, gotta get back to the family; cafeteria's over there, help yourself to anything. Might be some meatloaf left over from lunch Friday. You know, Fridays are meatloaf day, gotta love it. Anyway, light switch is by the door; might storm tonight so you'll want to stay in. Whiteouts are bad out here."

Kyle goes on about whiteouts, a warning we've heard a dozen times, with the addition of a story about a visitor who froze to death "just yards away from this here school," blinded by the blowing snow and unable to find the door. Since we're from California, everyone wants to make sure we don't take the Alaskan winter for granted. We don't.

The principal leaves, taking the kids with him; Tina and I head straight for the kitchen. Pilot bread, army surplus peanut butter and strawberry jam, dried-out meatloaf in the walk-in fridge and tins of Spam everywhere. Tina says, "You know, I'm not hungry. You eat, I'll unpack," and goes to the closet to untie the stilts, air our costumes and sort out the makeup.

I find a pan and start to fry up some Spam. "Throw me a head of lettuce out of the big duffle, OK?" Before we left San Francisco, Stephanie insisted that we pack a dozen heads of iceberg lettuce to give as presents — "Fresh veggies are gold this time of year" — and we've given most of them away to our favorite teachers and students in the first two villages. "Kyle didn't invite us to dinner so he doesn't get a present." The head Tina throws me is frozen solid.

After eating Spam sandwiches with cold lettuce, running the juggling act for our show tomorrow evening and finding the wrestling mats we'll need for acrobatics classes, Tina calls the top bunk and we say our good nights.

CHAPTER THREE

SCHOOL DAZE
Kwethluk

SLIPPING INTO MY SLEEPING BAG, I realize that I'm exhausted already, a bad sign less than halfway into this tundra tour. I might even be too tired to climb up to the top bunk if Tina invited me, but that's not happening. We're partners, not "partners," and it looks like that's how it's going to stay. I set my alarm and try to get comfortable in a bed that's only a few inches too short if I lie on the diagonal.

We spent our first week in Akiachak, a village about 15 air miles upriver from Bethel, and then went back to Bethel for a week in the "big city" schools before coming here to Kwethluk. The next two villages are longer flights but still on the Kuskukwim; our last two stops are way up on the Yukon River.

The tour schedule looked fine on paper — fly Sundays, teach Mondays and do our duet clown show on Monday nights; teach every kid in the school for the rest of the week and do another show on Friday afternoon with the kids performing. Saturdays we either fly back to Bethel or stay in the village to visit and rest up for the next week.

In San Francisco, this schedule seemed doable; it's a different story up here with weather delays, bad food and worse beds.

Our first village, Akiachak, welcomed us with the now standard swarm of kids followed by a wonderfully un-standard salmon dinner at the home of one of the teachers. Delicious food but awkward conversations about the struggles between Mormon missionaries, our host, and "those Moravians" who are trying to "steal Eskimo souls away from the true path." Apparently every white person in the village was there on a mission.

Most of Akiachak came to see us that Monday night, a few hundred folks sitting in the bleachers and on the gym floor to watch our clown show. In the part where Tina chases me into the audience, I "hid" by sitting in the lap of an old woman dressed in a *kuspuk*, the traditional Eskimo dress made of colorful gingham fabric and finished with lots of rickrack. The old woman grabbed my ass, hard, and said something in Yup'ik that got the biggest laugh of the evening. As I tried to get back to the stage, every old lady in the row copped a feel. They have strong fingers out here on the tundra.

At the end of the show, we got a long ovation that turned into a synchronized clap that got faster and faster. We exited behind the wrestling mats we'd upended to make a backdrop, gave each other a high five and started to pack up our equipment. It got very quiet. We peeked out to see the whole crowd sitting patiently, staring at our empty makeshift stage. We took another bow to scattered applause and exited again.

No one moved.

Tina grabbed her concertina, threw me three balls and said, "You juggle, I'll play." We did a quick encore and got some more applause but no one got up to go. We invited the kids to join us onstage and gave them scarves so they could show off the juggling they had learned in class that day. Then we walked through the audience shaking hands.

No one left.

Finally, we played another song, waved good-bye and went backstage. Eventually, folks started trickling out of the gym.

We found out later that Eskimo dancing is very popular in this area and the traditional way for an audience to reward a good dancer is by clapping in rhythm until they do their whole dance again, only faster. Superstar Eskimo dancers sometimes do a dozen encores, ending in a frenzied sweat. We clearly didn't get the message.

TUESDAY WAS ACROBATICS DAY, starting with a dozen fourth graders. I asked the kids to take off their shoes and line up. Nothing happened. 24 eyes just stared at me. I repeated myself, a little more slowly and with better articulation, "Please take off your shoes so we can do acrobatics on the mats."

Twelve kids stood completely still with blank looks on their faces.

Tina took off her shoes and did a string of fast cartwheels across the mats; the kids applauded and didn't move. A blond boy, clearly the son of a teacher, motioned for me to lean down so he could whisper in my ear, "Asking us to take off our shoes is like asking us to be naked. Can we leave our shoes on?" I stood up and said, "OK, please leave your shoes *on* and make two lines at this end of the mat."

Twelve kids raced to get in line, laughing and pushing.

We spent the day on forward rolls, backward rolls, cartwheels and, with the older ones, some two-person pyramids. The kids were agile and learned quickly so we added moving tricks, like two-person cartwheels and handstand overs. For the high school classes, we did big pyramids that started with a pair of bases on hands and knees, facing each other. The next two kids stood at right angles to the bases, facing each other with their hands on the bases' shoulders. The tower went up, each pair of kids standing on the last pairs' backs, making a structure that could safely, and impressively, include 10 kids.

For a treat at the end of each class, we brought out the tube of peacock feathers. Kids here are mesmerized by the delicate iridescence of the "eye" and love trying to balance the feathers on their hands, noses, elbows, feet.

ON WEDNESDAY SCHOOL was cancelled. The very first Kuskokwim 300 Sled Dog Race was running and the organizers had messed up the map at Akiachak — teams were supposed to turn right at a fork on the west end of town but the map showed them going straight. So the whole school, and most of the rest of the village, stood across the width of the river, a human blockade, stamping our feet to stay warm until a dog team appeared. Then we'd all point wildly until we heard the musher shouting, "Gee! Gee!" and the lead dog turned right down the fork. We'd cheer and wait for the next team.

After an hour of this, Tina said, "I'm freezing. Let's go back to the gym." I couldn't feel my toes so I started up the hill with her. We'd only gone a few yards when some kids shouted, "Susan, Susan!" One of the teachers called us back, "Susan Butcher's coming. She's the best woman musher in the world, if you don't count Libby Riddles."

We'd heard the story last year at the state fair, how Susan Butcher was supposed to be the first woman to win the Iditarod but the upstart Libby Riddles had beaten Butcher and a field of 35 other mushers to take that honor.

We turned just in time to see a team of nine huskies, the lead dog out in front with four pairs behind her, running up the hill to the village with an empty sled bouncing behind them. A woman in red coveralls was sprawled across the ice; the famous musher had turned but her dogs had gone straight.

A high school student drove his snowmobile up to Butcher; she jumped onto the seat behind him and they took off after the bouncing sled. Most of the kids ran after the snowmobile, and we tried to follow the kids. Dozens of village dogs were howling at the runaways. By the time Tina and I finally caught up, the action was over — Butcher was on her sled and the team was lined out, running back to the fork in the river. She'd lost 10 minutes max.

We went into the school and, after standing by the heater for a few minutes, Tina headed back out to find a craftswoman Stephanie had told her about, shopping for beaded earrings, Eskimo yoyos and sealskin masks. I joined a basketball game in the gym but managed to lose the ball every time I dribbled. I'm not a great player but I can do a layup, even on the cracked concrete of the Mission District playgrounds in San Francisco, where I usually play. On that smooth wood floor, I couldn't dribble worth a damn. The kids giggled every time the ball flew away from my hand. One of them finally told me that all gyms up here get frost heaves because it's too cold to completely insulate a hardwood floor. The kids knew every little bump and divot — I didn't.

Two women in *kusbuks* walked into the kitchen and the game stopped. The players dropped the ball and ran to roll out big metal triangles that unhinged into tables with benches on each side. Soon the gym was a cafeteria, full of children and the smell of mac and cheese. I sat down to eat and a bunch of elementary kids crowded in around me asking questions:

Are Tina and I married? No.
Am I married to someone else? No.
Where do I live? In an apartment in San Francisco.

What is an apartment?

The tweens and teens sat a little ways down the bench, trying to look wise and bored. The little guys started touching my hair and face.

How come your hair's curly?
Why is your nose so big?

I went into a long explanation of genetics, how my nose evolved from desert people and my hair is curly like my father's and grandfathers' while their hair is straight like their ancestors and their noses are flat, perfect for avoiding the tundra wind. The kids listened and touched my hair. They looked very serious. I was tempted to tell them more about genetics, about what happened to 6 million of my desert people and about their tundra ancestors' bodies getting ravaged by European germs and their culture being attacked by xenophobia.

I decided that was a bit heavy for a lunchtime chat.

"You were born with that hair?"

"And that nose?"

I could almost see their thought bubbles — a little baby with a giant nose and a mid-sized Jewish afro.

"Well, I had less of it when I was born but this is my natural hair. I don't do anything to make it curly."

Astonished little faces.

After a few moments, one of the teens, who had a head full of black curls, said, "Toni." The little kids all laughed.

"Good story. Born with curly hair. Yeah, I bet. That's funny." They pronounced "funny" with two syllables, a drawn out "u" on "fun" and a downward inflection on the "ny".

EARLY FRIDAY MORNING kids were playing basketball by seven and when the first bell rang the school was full. Starting with the kindergartners, we worked our way up to high school, class by class, creating a different act with each group: the little ones were circus animals, roaring and parading around; a scarf juggling act for the first grade, although they really wanted to wear the scarves as veils and pretend to get married; second graders balanced peacock feathers on their fingers, then on their elbows and finally on their noses. With the older students, we had acrobatic acts, human pyramids, stilt walking, ball and ring juggling and one unicycle rider.

At 3 pm, a group of teachers, parents and grandparents came into the gym to learn how to paint faces. White first, all over or just around the mouth and eyes. Use makeup sponges dipped in water, not too wet, and be careful not to touch any impetigo sores. Wait for the white to dry, about five minutes. Tell the kids not to touch it when it's wet.

Red is next, with a brush, on their cheeks and noses. With a different brush, finish with black accents on the eyebrows and to outline the white.

Don't do little pictures on their cheeks, even if they beg you for them. Clown makeup is not decoration; it is designed to exaggerate expressions.

Tell the kids that it will all wash off with soap and water after the show but that the red might stain a little.

Wash your sponges and brushes after every kid so you don't spread germs.

Tell them all not to sweat too much or get their faces wet before the show.

The kids started coming in before we were done with the makeup lesson, too excited to wait. They put on costumes from our supply of thrift store treasures and waited in line for makeup.

I finally drift off to sleep thinking about the Akiachak gym full of little clowns, thick black hair falling over their painted white skin, juggling, tumbling, walking stilts, balancing peacock feathers on their red noses and running wild, sweating and smiling.

Two grandmothers sit on folding chairs in the corner, watching the kids. They know them all, of course, but the whitened faces make it hard to tell who's who.

"Your grandson is good on those stilts." Martha speaks in Yup'ik with a slight accent she picked up as a teenager at Indian School.

"Over there? That's Eddie, Paula's grandson. You are even more blind than I thought." Anne Evens grew up in Akiachak and hasn't left, except for an occasional potlatch in a neighboring village, since she got back from Oklahoma. That was over 40 years ago. "My Jason is near the door, acting like his father after a few beers."

Martha looks where Anne is pointing and sees a gaggle of boys tripping on purpose, falling down and laughing. "I see him. He's making a fool of himself."

Anne says, "That's what the *gussak* clowns taught him to do, act like a drunk Eskimo." Martha makes clucking noises and shakes her head — white people never cease to amaze her. She came to the school today to paint faces so she could keep an eye on the clowns. She wanted to see what they were making the kids do. She never likes having strangers in the village, even the school teachers, and these clowns are worse than teachers.

CHAPTER FOUR

SHOWTIME
Kwethluk

THE RADIO ALARM GOES OFF, the glowing numbers read 6:30 and a breezy voice says, "...going to be a cool Monday in Kwethluk, folks. Negative 38 still air with winds up to 40 miles per hour. That means the wind chill'll get down to, let's see, negative 113. That's cold, my friends, real cold. Now remember: At these temperatures, human flesh freezes in 30 seconds. Well, that's the weather; now on to Trapline Chatter..."

One-hundred-and-thirteen degrees below zero? That doesn't seem possible.

Tina jumps down from the top bunk, "Cm'on, we gotta feel this. I bet we're never gonna be this cold again in our lives." My sleeping bag is toasty but I'm embarrassed to be such a wimp. We grab our cold weather gear and check each other for exposed skin before walking outside. We stand on the metal stairs and it doesn't seem unusually cold. Then a gust of wind makes me feel like I'm naked in a meat locker. We race back in. The huge heater hanging from the ceiling in the gym is blasting and it still takes a few minutes before we can take off our coats.

The weather eases up and the week in Kwethluk goes smoothly. Tina and I figured out our rhythms, our strengths and weaknesses, back in Akiachak and then we really got into our groove in the Bethel schools: I take the lead before lunch, with the little guys; Tina's pre-dawn rush to meet the cold notwithstanding, she isn't a morning person. Also, we have the younger grades in the morning and I learned to teach at a Mission District preschool, so I'm at home with the little ones. After lunch, Tina is in charge, charming and challenging the tweens and teens, getting instant cred with her handstands, deep backbends and rapid-fire flip-flops.

These kids spend a lot of time on ice and in boats, which gives them an edge learning circus skills. Here in Kwethluk, we've got George, a sophomore you'd mistake for a fifth grader, who learned to ride a unicycle Tuesday afternoon, pedaling across a classroom crowded with kids throwing scarves and practicing cartwheels. It took me a month to learn what George could do in an hour.

ON WEDNESDAY, after we're done working, Tina goes out to buy some souvenirs and I'm alone shooting free throws. Every clank on the rim or bounce on the floor echoes through the empty gym. In my head, I'm trying to picture the students from our last two villages, Akiachak and Bethel, but they're blurring together. I really loved those kids when I was with them and it feels like a betrayal to forget them as soon as I'm on to the next village. After a few more shots, I manage to put a few names to faces in my mind. But just a few.

Will I forget all the Eskimo kids I meet on this trip before I get back to San Francisco? How about the teachers? Will I forget Tina? Is that what I do, forget people I love as I race on to the next village or the next gig? But I do remember some people — my old best friend Butchie; my grandpa with his wattley neck; my Nana looking so tiny next to her giant son, my dad. I even have a few clear memories of Daddy, little snapshots — peeking through the door of his study to see his long back bent over his desk, feeling his scratchy cheek as he reads my brother and me a bedtime story — but not much more.

I put the basketball away and pick up some juggling clubs. I'd go for a walk if it wasn't so cold out, anything to keep from going down this road and getting all sad. It's the darkness and the weather and being out here in the middle of fucking nowhere, that's the problem. I don't get all morose when I'm home in the sunny Mission.

I'm still doing my three-club warm-up when Tina comes running into the gym, excited to show me a pair of sealskin earring shaped like tiny boots. Her excitement is contagious, getting me through our dinner of leftover mac and cheese and our evening rehearsal.

NOW, ON FRIDAY AFTERNOON, George is here in the gym on his unicycle, in makeup and costume, two hours before showtime. He's working on idling, riding backwards and pirouettes. He's been on that unicycle almost nonstop for four days.

The gym fills up and the performance is smooth: 60 kids showing off a combination of circus skills, clown makeup and cuteness. The ball jugglers and the human pyramid act are particularly good here in Kwethluk and the audience claps so fast for George that he does his unicycle act three times. We save him from doing it again by bringing all the kids up for a final bow.

After a lot of hugs, the gym is quiet and still.

Tina and I pull out a cafeteria table and sit down to write the report that Stephanie will send on to the Alaska Arts Council. We try to get it done right after the kids' show so 1) we don't forget what we did and 2) we don't have to think about it over the weekend. We stick to the basics — what we taught, what they did well, how many folks came to the final show and any issues we had with the school (food is always on the list).

We finish writing, eat some leftover meatloaf and are in the bunk beds by 9 pm. Jenny the Bush Pilot is picking us up to go back to Bethel in 12 hours and we have a lot of packing to do in the morning.

After trying to sleep for about an hour, I give up and get a glass of milk. What we *don't* say in the report is eating at me. Here in these Eskimo villages we're watching the painful assimilation of the Yup'ik world into mainstream America, cultural genocide in action. These kids are growing up in a twilight zone — their grandparents don't speak much English; they don't speak much Yup'ik. Whole families sit huddled together on one overstuffed chair watching "Dallas" beamed into their homes from the huge satellite dishes newly installed across the tundra. The suicide rate among high school boys is 10 percent, substance abuse is endemic, domestic violence is common.

Are Tina and I causing the same harm as "Dallas"?

These kids are Americans and they're dying to be in the TV version of America. But out here they still live something close to a traditional subsistence lifestyle — fishing, seal hunting, berry picking — then at school they study English, economics and history, from Hiawatha to the Holocaust, like every other American kid.

We are bringing joy to these villages and skills to these kids; how can we be on the wrong side of history? Sure, we're bringing American circus, with roots in Europe, not in Alaska; the clown acts have nothing to do with their lives, the makeup doesn't look like anything they've ever seen. But they take to the circus skills like skates on ice.

I'm sure we can do better. Maybe we should weave in some Yup'ik stories or use some traditional patterns in the makeup, anything to help link the circus we're bringing up from San Francisco to the real life of tundra villages.

Cozy back in my sleeping bag, I'm trying to imprint the faces of the Kwethluk kids in my mind, Eskimo faces painted clown white. I've already forgotten some of them. Tina and I are fooling ourselves that we're different than "Dallas." As I fall asleep, I have a nightmare image of us as the circus S.S., marching over the tundra in flap shoes instead of jackboots.

George Mackie can't sleep. He can still feel the unicycle seat between his legs. He wants to run over to the gym and ride all night, ride even with no one watching and no one applauding.

Rolling on that wheel, feeling the muscles in his legs, turning his hips so he stays on balance — he feels whole, like he and the unicycle were separated at birth but now they are back together and he is the man he's supposed to be. George has read about centaurs and he gets the idea that he is a modern-day version, half man and half wheel.

George sits up in bed. He relives the audience urging him to ride again and again, faster and faster. Then he thinks about the girls after the show, the ones who have always called him Shorty and Baby Georgie. They looked at him with eyes that made him shiver. He'd only seen that look from the side, watching the girls watching the strong boys wrestle or the tall boys shoot hoops. And the old ladies who always pinch his arms and say, "You need to eat more *akutaq*," those same grandmas kissed him and smothered his face into their sealskin *kusbuks*.

George decides he'll buy his own unicycle when this one flies off with the clowns. He misses his bottom half already. He wonders how much a unicycle costs. He wonders which catalog carries them and if he can somehow find enough money. Then he imagines his new unicycle nestled between huge bags of diapers and kegs of cooking oil in the shipping container that arrives in Kwethluk every year, a few weeks after breakup.

CHAPTER FIVE

PAIN
Kwethluk

6:30 AM. "…BEAUTIFUL SATURDAY out on the coast with highs around zero. Great day for a picnic but you still gotta wear your mittens, kittens. Here in Bethel, it is socked in with gusts up to 15 miles per hour. Mail planes might not get out 'til Monday so don't stand by the landing strip all day waiting for that package.

"Alright, we're ready for Trapline Chatter. Our first one is to Sally in Unalakleet: 'Stuck in Bethel, please feed the dogs. From Ted.'

"This one's to Danny in Kotlik: 'Make breakfast and help your brother get ready for wrestling, I'll be home after I find a new belt for the Sno-Go. From Mom.'

"Here's a good one: 'To the clowns in Kwethluk: Sorry to call you that but I forgot your names. Anyway, I can't fly out of Bethel today, socked in, but I'll try to pick you up tomorrow morning. Hope you listen to Trapline Chatter so you don't wait for me all day. From your pilot, Jenny.'

"Got that, clowns? Now this one goes out to the Alexi family in Stebbins…"

"Tina, you can go back to sleep. We're stuck here 'til tomorrow." There's no sound from the top bunk so I doze for a while before getting up, eating a PBJ on pilot bread and trying a few new juggling tricks.

By the time Tina's up and breakfasted, I'm bored with dropping a five-club flash and ready to pack.

We have just finished wrapping the last stilt bundle when Kyle Stern, the principal, comes in.

"I just heard from Lucy Beaver over at the store — you know the store has the only phone in the village and some days you have to wait an hour or more to use it. Anyway, Lucy Beaver came over to my house a few minutes ago saying that Stephanie called her to say your plane can't make it out of Bethel today. Socked in. Lucy heard it on Trapline Chatter this morning and figured you already knew but when Stephanie called, she decided she should come tell me. I told Lucy that you're from San Francisco, you don't listen to Trapline Chatter, you could care less about who's fixing their snow machine and whose dogs got sick. Anyway, your plane should make it tomorrow and Stephanie said to go straight to Kipnuk, not back to Bethel 'cause you're likely to get stuck in Bethel tomorrow and not make it to Kipnuk 'til Monday."

He finally takes a breath and sees the pile of equipment at his feet.

"You're all packed; that's good. Just have to move your stuff out of the gym before wrestling practice at three. You might want to stay inside; it's not too bad now but whiteouts are dangerous here in the bush…"

And he's off again with the warning about whiteouts, including the story of the guy who froze to death "just two feet from that door *right there*."

"Get yourself some meatloaf, left over from yesterday's lunch. You know Fridays are meatloaf days. Were you here last Friday? Anyway, ya gotta love meatloaf days." And he walks out.

Tina flicks her thumbnail from behind her top teeth, "*Mangiare la merda!*" (Tina studied in Italy back in the day.) "I'll bet Kyle and all the little Sterns wouldn't dream of eating leftover meatloaf. 'Meatloaf days, gotta love it.' If he'd of said another word, I'd'a turned him into meatloaf." She grabs a stilt bundle and starts to drag it back to the storeroom. "Let's get this stuff out of the way and work on the act 'til the wrestlers get here."

WE'RE RUNNING OUR LAST TRICK, a seven-clubs pile-up — Tina catching all seven clubs in her arms, one at a time, in rhythm — when the wrestlers start coming in. They cheer and ask us to do it again. After a few more pile-ups, the boys go change into their singlets and pull out the mats. Now it's our turn to watch them as they grapple and hinge each other until someone is flat on his back, pinned. They are fast and strong.

When practice is over, about five o'clock, we walk the wrestlers to the door, thinking we might get out of the school for a few minutes. It's completely dark and the wind is howling so we go right back in.

"Hey, the mats are out; wanna work your flip-flop?"

Tina's been spotting my back handspring since before we left San Francisco. I've got a good front handspring, landing soft and straight, but when I try to go backwards, I always twist to my left. A guy my size flying through the air is surprising, and flying through the air backwards would be even better.

I stand at the edge of the mat and Tina stands behind me with her hands on my back. She's almost a foot shorter than me. Without saying anything, I bend my legs, lower my arms and then quickly push off with everything I've got, trying to go straight backwards over Tina's head. She stops me mid-flight and pushes me back to standing.

"Good, good. You didn't twist much. Again."

After a few more of these warm-ups, Tina goes on my left side with her right hand on my back and her left hand behind my thighs. I flip back onto my hands and then whip my feet over to standing — with a lot of help from Tina. "Good, good. Nice and light, no twist. Again." A few more and each time Tina is spotting less until she's just safety spotting; her hands are there in case anything goes wrong but I'm completely on my own.

This is the closest I've come to doing a flip-flop. Tina is talking me through, keeping me focused and channeling my excitement into execution. "You got it. Do one on your own." And I do, a little too heavy on the landing but no twist. High fives and then, "Again."

Two more times and I'm feeling it, feeling light, feeling strong, feeling straight.

"Again."

Now I'm flat on my face on the hardwood floor, screaming in pain, holding my left elbow.

Tina is kneeling beside me. "You OK? You twisted on that one." I manage to blurt out, "Ice. Please." I see a scared look flash across Tina's face before she runs into the kitchen.

"No ice in the freezer. Sorry."

My elbow is already visibly swollen, a bad sign. "Outside. Tundra. Snow."

"Oh. Duh. Sorry. Be back in a minute."

I gingerly roll over, holding my left arm tight to my body. The floor is cold. I'm alone, lying on the hardwood. All my bravado, all my Road Warrior courage melts away and I'm scared. I can feel the flat white tundra stretching out in every direction. I think about my apartment 2,000 miles away. I think about the room I grew up in, with the long, skinny bed and chartreuse walls. I am suddenly so homesick I sob.

Tina comes back with a plastic bag full of snow and presses it on my elbow. She sits down, still holding the bag, and lifts my head into her lap with her free hand. She wipes my cheek. We're quiet for a while; I'm not crying any more; the pain has dulled and I can smell Tina's skin. Now I'm trying not to think about how we'll manage the next month with only three good arms between us.

CHAPTER SIX

WHITEOUT
Bethel and Kipnuk

"I WOULD LET YOU FLY 'ER if your arm wasn't so bum." Bucky, the mail plane pilot, sounds genuinely sorry. "Anyway, we'll be in Bethel right quick; it may be Monday morning but ain't no rush hour up here like you got in San Fran. And no waiting for air traffic control like at SFO." Bucky laughs for a long time before snorting to a stop and saying, "Hope you get to see a doc at the hospital — it's supposed to be for native folks, you know. With that schnozzola on you, you'll never pass." Another laughing fit, another snort.

We're quiet for a few seconds, too long for Bucky. "How'd you mess up that elbow, anyway? Fall off a Sno-Go?" I give him the shorthand version of my flip-flop accident and he says, "Bummer, man" then launches into a long story about hurting his elbow when he worked on the pipeline up in Prudhoe Bay.

I stare out the plane window at the white.

When Jenny came to pick us up in Kwethluk yesterday, we were a sad little circus; my arm was in an improvised sling and Tina had been up half the night puking. Tainted meatloaf or the flu, we weren't sure. Seeing us, the only thing Jenny said was "Bad move, Clown Boy," and she sulked the rest of the flight to our fourth village.

When we met the principal of Kipnuk School, a John Wayne look-alike with Mr. Rogers' sweetness, he did a good job of hiding his disappointment. "We'll walk right over to the health aide's house and get you something for your tummy. But she can't do anything for that arm, I'm afraid. The mail plane comes early-squirrely tomorrow so you can get into Bethel, let the real doctors work their magic. Don't worry about your show; I'll just move it to Tuesday night. By then, you'll both be shipshape."

Whatever the health aide gave Tina stopped the puking but she still felt like shit this morning. I felt terrible leaving her to teach alone, but I have to get my elbow looked at — it's the size and color of an eggplant.

Bucky is still talking "…had that arm in a cast for a month but it didn't slow me down. Anyhoo, beautiful downtown Bethel coming right up." He slides the plane onto the well-plowed runway. "Let me pull up so the boys can unload the mail; you can hop out after I secure the props. You do not want to get caught up in one of these bad boys, turn you into chopped liver faster than you can say, 'Bucky warned me.'" Laugh, snort. "Be in the lobby by 2 pm sharp if you want a ride back to Kipnuk."

I'VE BEEN SITTING for a couple of hours on a flimsy plastic chair in the hospital waiting room, staring at old yellow linoleum. A nurse has called my name three times, but each time she asked me to sit back down so they could deal with an emergency in from one of the villages. My arm aches. It could be serious. I might not be able to work and if I lose this job I'll be broke; I won't be able to pay for an acting class, much less a year at Dell'Arte International theater school. I'll never get a theater gig without training and I'll never get another circus gig with a bum arm. It's depressing. I try not to go down that road.

The nurse calls me again and fourth time's a charm; I get in to see Dr. Dent.

"Call me Roger 'cause I'm not really a doc. Medic, Vietnam, '68 to '71. See a lot of the same things up here as I saw in Nam. How'd you do that arm?"

I tell the story again and Roger does some pushing and prodding. "It's OK, no fracture but you tore the ligaments pretty good. Scar tissue is your enemy; if you let it form up, you lose mobility. Permanently. Gotta move it a lot."

I straighten and flex my arm a couple of times. It hurts.

"Gently."

I slowly move my forearm up and down.

"Yeah, that's it."

I get an idea and mime a juggling pattern. "Alright, yeah, that'll work. Juggling as physical therapy. Pretty good. But no flips, OK?" I agree but tell him we've got a show tomorrow night. "Just wear a sling, maybe something a little nicer than that rag you came in with. Six weeks minimum for recovery, permanent damage depends on you. Let pain be your boss — it hurts, you quit. And keep it warm."

Before I leave, he tosses me three rolled ace bandages and I do a little juggling act. "Yep, that'll work just fine. Juggling as P.T. Love it. Hey, P.T. Barnum!" I leave him laughing at his own joke.

Walking back to the airport, I stop by a store to buy a yard of red fabric for my show sling. Even with the wind up and snow starting to fall, I'm in the terminal with time to spare. There are only two airline counters, Wien Air Alaska and Ryan Air, plus a bunch of charters. I overhear a pilot telling a family that they'll have to stay another day in Bethel because the weather is getting too bad to fly. I'm glad I'm on the mail plane, which is bigger than most charters, and flying with Bucky, who is supposed to be the best bush pilot around.

A few minutes later, I see Bucky walking toward the front door. "Bucky, ready to go when you are."

"Oh, man, sorry. Weather's up, no mail run. I can drive you over to Stephanie's place if you want. Used to be a hotel so I'm sure she's got room for ya."

I turn down the ride and Bucky leaves. I haven't mentioned this hospital run, or my injury, to Stephanie. She'll find out when we're back in Bethel after our week in Kipnuk and by then I'll have proved that I can do the gig one-handed. I can't get sent home now and leave Tina to do the second half of the tour alone. And I need the money. My application to the theater school is in the mail and if they take me for this fall, they'll want a deposit pretty soon. If they haven't accepted me by the time we get home, I'm going to send one of our Alaska Council reports and some of the pictures that Tina's been taking. Who else has "circus snow tour" on their résumé? They'll have to accept me and I'll have to send them a deposit.

Even if I wasn't worried about telling Stephanie, I still need to get back to Kipnuk tonight so I'll be ready to teach tomorrow morning.

No one will take me.

"We're closing up 'til this storm passes."

"Too much snow."

"This is Alaska, son. The weather is your schedule."

The airport is emptying out and I'm starting to get desperate when a small man in a bulky camouflage coat and a flap-eared fur hat comes in from the tarmac covered in snow. He stops to stomp his boots and I ask him for a ride to Kipnuk. "Sure. Gotta go to Goodnews Bay and it's kind of on the way. You ready now?" "Ready." "Okay, wait here, let me take a leak, gas up and we're good to go."

It's really storming when we take off. I tell the pilot, whose name is Ken, the whole story of why I need to get back to Kipnuk tonight. He knows Stephanie — everyone knows Stephanie — and promises to wait to bill her for the flight until next month. I thank him and he stops talking to concentrate on keeping the little plane going southwest, through the storm, above the Kuskokwim River.

After about an hour, he turns north up the Bering coast to Kipnuk and somehow finds the landing strip — it looks like one big snowdrift to me. We bump to a stop. "Better get going while you can still see the village." I climb out even before the propeller stops and head for the faint outline of the school about a half a mile away. As soon as I'm clear, Ken taxies forward and crashes right into a snow bank. I keep walking.

"Hey, help me push her out, OK? You've still got a few minutes before it's a full whiteout." I run back and we each take a wing. The plane is amazingly light and we roll it back easily, even though I've only got one working arm. "Thanks."

I start walking toward the school again, which is now just a blur, and turn back to see Ken take off almost straight up and immediately disappear into the clouds. I listen for the crash, don't hear it and start running.

"WHERE HAVE YOU BEEN hide-and-seeking yourself?" The principal wiggles his finger right under my nose. "Tina's spent the whole day teaching all by her lonesome, and on a bad tummy to boot. I thought you were stuck in Bethel but now I see you've been here right along. It's not nice to play hooky, especially when you're the teacher." There is real anger in his voice but I'm too relieved to care.

"Just got in. From Bethel. Landed a few minutes ago. Ran over from the strip."

"Just now? In this whiteout?" The color drains from his John Wayne face, his mouth opens and closes a few times. I excuse myself to go find Tina.

This scene repeats itself a dozen times over the next hour — the people who believe I landed in the middle of the storm are glad that I'm alive; most folks think I'm lying because they know that no one, not even Ken, would fly in this weather. At least Tina is glad to see me and too sick to care about when I flew where. I make her some bullion and put her to bed early.

The village rumor mill is fast so by the next morning everyone seems to have an opinion about me — crazy flier or low-down liar. Liar is the preferred option.

CHAPTER SEVEN

NAKED CLOWN TIME
Kipnuk and Bethel

OUR CLOWN DUET ON TUESDAY EVENING is barely passable, with some improvised three-hand juggling patterns and no partner acrobatics. The rest of the week in Kipnuk isn't much better — my arm aches, everyone thinks I'm a liar and Tina's still sick. The only good times are in the evenings when I get to pamper Tina, who seems to like it.

The kids' show Friday afternoon is OK but they haven't learned as much as the students in the first three villages and it is painfully obvious, at least to us. When the gym finally clears out, we feel guilt mixed with relief that we survived the week.

Half the village comes out on Saturday morning to help us load the plane. They are embarrassingly grateful and treat Tina like a wounded celebrity. Jenny, decked out in new hot-pink coveralls, is a little friendlier but she still doesn't let me fly the Cessna.

In the converted hotel back in Bethel, over a feast of salmon with fresh salad supplied by a couple of opera singers who just arrived from Seattle, Stephanie scolds us for not calling her when I got hurt. I make apologetic sounds between bites but Stephanie is on a tear. "And you flew back in the middle of a storm, with Ken White no less, the most crazy-assed bush pilot on the Delta. If he sends me a bill I'm not paying; damn fool trying to kill my artists." I listen, look contrite and eat. Stephanie finally calms down: "Well, we've got two more groups going to Kipnuk this year, including these singers, so I guess I'm glad you made it work. Hate to have villages start cancelling programs."

The opera singers, a young blond couple who each outweigh me, are wolfing down the salmon at the same rate as we are devouring the salad; it looks like Tina's stomach is back on track. The singers give us greasy smiles and Stephanie says, "Who's up for some wine and a sauna?"

She pulls out a couple of bottles of Napa Valley pinot noir, smuggled in from California, and we make quick work of them. "Ready for a steam? It's a *gussak* sauna, not as hot as the *maqiviks* out in the villages but it'll get you sweating." The opera couple begs off, worried about their vocal cords, but Tina and I are game. We slip on our boots, untied, and follow the beam of Stephanie's flashlight as she leads us out back to a small wooden shed. There is smoke pouring out of a pipe sticking through the roof.

The shed is divided into two tiny rooms, one for changing and one for sweating. In the changing room, Stephanie strips down to nothing in one smooth move and slides through the door into the sauna. "Get in here, it's nice and toasty." Tina laughs and says, "Naked clown time!" and strips down, too. Tina is small, with a gymnast's body and not an ounce of false modesty. She catches me staring and does a quick little Betty Boop move before following Stephanie in. I'm slower to undress and carefully hang my clothes on the wooden pegs halfway up the wall. I slip into the sauna and sit on the wooden bench in the only open space, between the two women.

It's awkward sitting naked squeezed thigh-to-thigh between my boss and my clown partner but the thick steam starts working on our muscles and we settle into a sauna trance. The heat feels great on my bad arm and I straighten it out almost as far as it goes, a first since the accident. As I'm folding my arm back up, I accidently rub Tina's breast. I turn to apologize but she leans into my arm, gives me a wicked grin and wiggles her eyebrows.

Stephanie starts to talk, so softly I can hardly make out the words. Tina leans even farther in to hear.

"The next village is different. In a good way. More traditional. Everyone speaks Yup'ik." She swallows the final 'k' with a short growl, the correct pronunciation. "They speak English, too, but Yup'ik is the first language. They've got an Eskimo teacher in the school; not too many Eskimo teachers out here, mainly white missionaries. You know, you've met them. But you'll like Paul Paul."

"Did you say Paul Paul?" Tina asks, now practically lying across my chest. Her body is hot and sweaty.

"That's his real name — there are a lot of Pauls here in the bush, a big family. I guess Paul Paul's folks weren't feeling real creative when they named him."

"OK. Got it. Paul Paul." Tina leans back, mouths "Paul Paul" and crosses her eyes. I stifle a giggle. We've become a couple of 15-year-olds, flirting while we pretend to listen to our teacher…who is naked. We're naked, too, and it is hot in here.

"The village was called *Ekvicuaq*." The final syllable comes out of Stephanie's mouth like a cat choking up a hairball. "The missionaries couldn't pronounce it so now it's Eek."

"Eek?" We both laugh and Stephanie keeps talking, "Chuna McGinty's from Eek. You heard of him yet?"

"No, ma'am" and Tina squeezes my thigh to keep from laughing.

"The one that got away. Chuna's an artist and singer and dancer. Raised by his grandma, very traditional woman."

Tina is now rubbing my thigh, making it hard for me to listen to the boss but I'm not about to stop Tina so I try to multitask. "Did Chuna leave Eek?" The last word comes out of my mouth a little higher than I had planned.

"He went off to Fairbanks, to the university, and now he's making a name for himself as an artist in the lower forty-eight."

Tina's hand comes off my thigh and taps me on the shoulder. I turn and see that her face is purple-red and dripping wet. She's not smiling anymore. She tilts her head toward the door; I nod and ask Stephanie, "Are any of Chuna's relatives still in Eek?" to cover Tina's exit.

"A lot of McGintys still in Eek; Chuna's dad is the janitor at the school, which is like being the mayor in an Eskimo village."

I scoot over on the bench to give Stephanie some room and we sit there quietly for a few minutes. I hear the outside door close and hope that Tina's OK.

"We'll meet Chuna's dad on Monday then. Good. Chuna doesn't go back to Eek at all?"

"No, he doesn't. Complicated scene with the family. But get friendly with his dad; he's The Man in Eek. Paul Paul will take care of you, too. He's a good guy."

I'm getting seriously cooked by now so I say, "Be back in a minute," run into the changing room and then right out the door and jump face-first into a snowbank with my bad arm held up in the air. The snow feels great. I consider running into the house to find Tina but decide I should get my clothes first. I go back into the sauna and almost slam right into Stephanie, half-dressed just inside the door. I stand in front of her, naked and dripping snow.

"You might not want to make a habit of that — it's around 190 degrees in the sauna and negative 20 outside so you're dropping over 200 degrees in an instant, which can stop your heart." She pulls on her pants, slips on her boots and walks past me, yelling over her shoulder, "The flashlight's on the bench."

I stand for another moment, waiting to see if my heart will stop. It doesn't. I get dressed quickly, grab the flashlight and go back into the old hotel, praying that Tina hasn't cooled down entirely.

It's dark and quiet in the front hall. The singers are in their room, I assume; Tina might be washing up and Stephanie is probably in her room. The house feels abandoned. Now I'm a 15-year-old ditched by his friends. Using the flashlight, I find the stairs.

I'll go up to my room, change into PJs and find Tina, at least to say goodnight and at most...

"Boo!"

I drop the flashlight and trip down a couple of steps. Tina, standing over me dressed in my parka with the wolf tail covering her face, howls with laughter. I stammer, "Damn, you scared me." Doors open down the hall and Tina calls out in her best teacher voice, "Everything's OK. Good night."

I go down a few more stairs to get the flashlight and when I get climb up, the hallway is empty. Tina's gone. My room is the last on the left so I walk slowly down the hall, swinging the light beam back and forth and get to my door without incident.

Maybe Tina's had her fun and gone to bed. I hope not.

I open my door and switch on the light. Tina is standing in the middle of my room still wearing my parka. She whispers, "boo" and lets the parka slide off her arms and onto the floor. She's naked. I open my mouth and stare. Tina takes one step forward and jumps onto me, wrapping her gymnast legs around my torso. I hold her thigh with my good arm and we kiss long and hard.

CHAPTER EIGHT

EEK
Bethel and Eek

SUNDAY MORNING. Don't need to get up. Don't need to be at the airport until later. Sheets are tangled around my feet. My head aches.

I open my eyes a slit and see a big toe a few inches from my face. It's floating in midair. My eyes focus and I follow the toe to a foot and then down to a calf and then a knee, thigh, red cotton underwear, a white tank top and then Tina's head balanced upside down on the floor surrounded by a puddle of curly red hair. I hear "good morning" and it sounds like Tina's voice. I mutter "morning" and try to sit up.

Tina pushes up out of her headstand into a handstand and then snaps her feet to the ground. I groan as her landing shakes the bed. She's standing over me, smiling.

"You were a whole lot friskier last night. Did the pinot take it out of you or was it me?"

Even in my addled state I know the correct answer is "It was you." Tina smiles and hands me a mug of coffee that was too hot to drink about 30 minutes ago. It's thick stuff and the caffeine works its magic almost immediately.

"You're a wild woman this morning."

"Just this morning?"

"No, you were a wild woman last night, too, but I could keep up with you then."

"Well, you tried to keep up." She laughs and I want to jump up and kiss her but I can't get my legs out of the sheets.

"I'm going downstairs to eat — I'm starving. Coming with?"

"I'll be down in a minute."

Tina pulls on her sweatpants, gives me a kiss on the cheek and opens the door.

I say, "Hey, I thought you weren't a morning person."

"All depends on what happens the night before." And she's off to breakfast.

By the time I get downstairs everyone has finished eating and they're sipping coffee in the living room. I make some toast, pour a fresh cup and join them. Stephanie flashes me a knowing look but doesn't say anything about last night. She is giving the singers advice on teaching in the villages.

"You're artists bringing a world of music to these tiny, isolated towns but don't forget that there's already music out here, Yup'ik music. This program is designed to build a bridge between the *gussak* world and the Yup'ik world." I'm wondering what this means for our circus program when Tina asks the couple to sing one of their pieces. They oblige and we're transported to La Scala.

On my second refill I start to feel normal again — pinot noir, sauna and Tina really took it out of me. Tina is focused on the singers, not me, and I wonder if she's regretting last night. We did break a cardinal rule of clowning: never sleep with your partner. But maybe that rule needs an update: never sleep with your partner unless you're out in the middle of frozen nowhere and things are rough and you're not going to let a little sex mess up your act and…

"OK, time to get to the airport. Jenny wants to leave at one, drop the circus in Eek and then take the opera on to Kwigillingok." Stephanie looks at me. "We could leave a little later but you clowns have all that crap that we have to load into the van and then unload and load onto the plane. Why can't you be like the singers — some sheet music and a portable keyboard? You don't see them making me schlepp stilts and unicycles and whatever the hell else you have in all those bags." She's smiling but her eyes are hard. Maybe she knows the cardinal rule of clowns.

THE TENOR GETS THE FRONT SEAT in the Cessna and the soprano sits behind him, leaving Tina and me squished together behind Jenny.

We're back to being teenagers, trying not to bump the pilot while doing everything we can to make each other giggle or moan. Luckily Jenny wants to hear some opera, so our shenanigans are covered by duets from *Roméo et Juliette*.

When we're done unloading on the runway in Eek, Jenny punches my shoulder and gives me a wink before jumping back in the Cessna and flying the singers off to Kwigillingok.

Paul Paul is waiting to greet us the moment we step into the school. He's a short, pleasantly plump man with an open face framed by straight black bangs. "Welcome to Eek, my friends. Good to see you. Stephanie has been singing your praises. Hey, nice ruff, I like the wolf tail. Who made it for you?" I tell him I made it myself and Paul whistles through his teeth, "You Californians, you're really crafty."

Tina starts to pick up a duffel but Paul stops her. "Leave everything here in the hall; the kids will put it away." Tina drops the duffel and we start to take off our coats. "You might want to leave your coats on. Robin invited you over to lunch. Are you hungry?" I'm always hungry these days, maybe from the cold, maybe because the school food is so bad. "Let's go then, she's waiting."

Tina takes our last head of iceberg lettuce, brown and frozen, out of her bag, and Paul leads us out the back door. "Robin lives on the other side of the village…watch out for the ice on the stairs here. You know about Robin, right?" We admit we don't. "She's a teacher from Connecticut but she lives in Eek, almost five years now. Has a house in the village. Married William McGinty, Chuna McGinty's brother."

Tina is holding me tight, ostensibly to keep from slipping on the ice.

Paul adds, "John McGinty's son," as if that settles everything. Tina and I both say "Oh" and walk arm in arm through the snow behind our host.

"Chuna's away in the lower forty-eight but you'll meet John McGinty tomorrow at school."

We all go into the kitchen of a two-room wood-frame house that smells of seal oil. There is a cloth covering a corner of the bedroom which we now know hides the honey bucket. Robin and William greet us with village-style handshakes. They are the first "mixed" couple we've met — she is short with straight brown hair nearly down to her lumbar curve, a strong jaw and lots of freckles; he is almost my height, rail thin with short-cropped black hair and soft eyes. They are both dressed in jeans and red plaid insulated LL Bean shirts.

Tina gives Robin the pathetic head of lettuce; they laugh and are fast friends. After a few minutes of chatting, Paul Paul heads back to school with William, who is the special education aide for the high school, saying they need to prep for next week's classes. I quietly eat wilted lettuce with salmon strips, ropes of smoked fish that are rich, oily and delicious, as the two women talk about their East Coast childhoods. I'm happy to watch Tina and listen to how she moved west and leveraged her grade-school gymnastics into a circus career. Robin talks about using her teaching credential to lead a life of adventure, including stints at schools in Nepal, South Korea, Hawai'i and finally here in Eek.

Over cups of hot Lipton's, Tina gets Robin to talk about her horrible first year on the tundra, about how the other teachers treated the students as damaged goods, about trying to fit in but being shunned by both the white folks for "going native" and the villagers for being another *gussak* who wants to play Eskimo for a year or two before taking her fat paycheck back to the lower forty-eight to buy a big house with central heating and a lawn.

Robin tells us about being home in Connecticut after that first year and finding herself thinking about William way too much and then about changing her plane ticket to get back to Eek a week early and volunteering to help with the special ed program so they could be together. Robin's second year sounds like "Romeo and Juliet on the Frozen Tundra" with John McGinty stepping in at the last minute to turn the story from a tragedy to comedy, complete with a traditional Eskimo wedding. Once Robin moved away from the teachers' housing into William's place in the village proper, she started to be accepted by the Yup'ik folks and rejected by the teachers.

"This year has been pretty good since most of my colleagues are new — the average stay for a teacher out here is a couple or three years. I've got seniority, I'm a given. Of course, they all hear the gossip about me before they arrive, the crazy white girl who married a local and pretends to be an Eskimo. But when they get here, I make sure to help them get settled, meet local folks and try to knock some of the more overt racist ideas out of their heads. It's hard, especially with the missionaries, but this village is stronger than most — the language is alive, the traditional stories are still told." Robin gets up to refill our teacups. "I've been talking a blue streak; what about you two?"

Tina gives me a look like, "Well, what about us two?" I look at the floor, sip my tea and finally say, "I better head back to the school to unpack; we've got a long day tomorrow." Tina rolls her eyes, Robin stifles a laugh and I scoot out the door.

William and Paul walk to the school in silence. William is trying to piece his wife back together in his mind, trying to put the Robin who suddenly appeared when their visitors arrived back together with the Robin who is his wife. It's not easy. Lower Forty-Eight Robin's voice is louder, her accent is harsher and she moves faster than his Wife Robin. This new Robin is exciting and exotic and a little scary to William in the way that strange young women are to men from small towns.

It's the other woman, Tina, who made his wife disappear. A picture of Tina comes into William's head — small, compact body, open, smiling face with wild copper-colored hair. He's sure she liked him at first sight — she gave him a flirtatious look — but then Tina looked away and handed that rotten lettuce to Robin. It cast a witch's spell — his wife disappeared and another *gussak* lady appeared in her body.

William sighs loudly and Paul looks back over his shoulder. William smiles and Paul smiles back. They keep walking through the snow. William wonders if Paul saw it too, saw the presto change-o magic act that Tina did on Robin. Paul is married to an Eskimo woman from Shaktoolik, way up north. She never disappears, not like Robin does.

They walk up the metal steps and into the warm school. As they take off their gear, William tells himself that Robin needs to become her old self, her lower forty-eight self, from time to time. He reminds himself that she changes every fall when the white teachers arrive but is back to her real self, her Eskimo self, as soon as she gets home from school every day. He hopes she'll be his wife again when he gets home tonight.

CHAPTER NINE

TUNDRA GHOST
Eek

IT'S DARK AND COLD as I try to find my way back to the school from Robin and William's house. I can almost hear the women behind me, laughing and sipping tea. Amazing — one night with Tina and we're already an "item." The Cute Clown Couple of the Tundra. I've had a crush on Tina for years but going from flirting to old married couple in 24 hours was never my fantasy. A home movie plays in my head: decades of identical school shows, Tina and me, in small towns across America, each audience getting a little smaller and each show getting a little duller. Then the image of Tina slipping out of my parka last night makes me smile and get a little warmer.

I'm not on the main road anymore. I've lost track of the lights in the gym. There's a house in front of me, the wall of a house, no door. I go around the right side and the darkness explodes with howling. I hear a chain snap taut and feel hot breath near my face. I fall backwards in the snow. The dark is full of barking and yipping and chains snapping. I crawl to my feet and take a step forward only to be body slammed back to the ground. I lie still for a moment before I smell dog breath and my face is covered with a huge tongue, licking and slurping. I laugh, sit up and nuzzle the sled dog who is now trying to climb into my lap.

I've stumbled into a musher's yard full of dozens of sled dogs chained to tiny houses. They are going crazy, thrilled that someone is visiting them and maybe even bringing dinner. I go dog to dog, petting them and trying to stay on my feet, getting licked and rubbed and even peed on — these are outside dogs, no inside manners at all.

NOW THE DOGS ARE WHIMPERING behind me, the lights of the

school are in front of me and I'm a happy mess. I love dogs. When I was a baby, we had a big black Labrador named Bray. My folks got the dog right after their honeymoon and they named him *B'reishit*, the first word of the Hebrew Bible — "In the beginning..." *B'reishit* got shortened to Bray and family lore has it that my first solid food was kibbles out of his dog bowl. Going into a store, my mother would say, "Watch the baby" and Bray would put his front paws on my stroller and stare at me until my mom got back. He would have mauled anyone who tried to touch me.

Bray continued to love me even as I grew enough teeth to bite his tail and even after I invented the game "Pull the balls, hear the dog yelp." But he started biting other kids, even though it was me who was torturing him, and he had to be put down.

I find the front door of the school and, just as I reach for the handle, I hear a howl from off in the dark, then another one and another. The sled dogs are calling me. I turn around and a small patch of blue in the sky catches my eye. The Northern Lights! I watch in awe as the blue glow grows and pulses, becoming a curtain of yellow and green, even a little purple at the top. Now it's two curtains covering half the sky. The dogs are howling, the huge sky is bursting with light and I howl back. It gets quiet for a moment before the dogs go crazy. I stand at the top of the stairs, howling with the dogs and staring at the sky, until the cold chases me inside.

Back in the gym, I change into my second pair of pants and a clean shirt. I'm heading back out for more aurora borealis when I notice that the lights are on in the room next door to the gym. I peek in to see Paul Paul and William sitting in tiny chairs, chatting in Yup'ik and laughing. They look up when I walk in and Paul switches to English, "You found your way back; you must have good night vision. The women are still visiting?" I nod and then look around — *ulus, mukluks* and *kusbuks* are displayed on tables around the room and the walls are covered with Yup'ik masks. I say, "This is a lot different than the other classrooms I've seen out here."

"Eskimo kids learn a lot of stuff in school, stuff that is important. We're Americans, right? But we're also not Americans." Paul walks over to a big map on the wall behind his desk and points out the distances.

"Alaska is only 55 miles from Russia and almost 1,000 miles from the Lower Forty-Eight. We're far away from most of you. We love you and all but we don't live like you. Our kids learn a lot of stuff about things they will never see, things that you see every day but, you know, we're out here on the tundra. So I bring in Alaskan things, Yup'ik things, so they can see a little of their world here at school."

He takes a mask down and hands it to me. It is half white and half black, divided from forehead to chin, with a black circle the size of a big cookie around the eye on the white side and a matching white circle on the black side. Yin and yang. Each eye circle has little dots of the opposite color around its circumference. There are three black lines coming down from the lower lip to the bottom of the white chin and three matching white lines on the black side. It is mysterious and a little scary.

Paul laughs. "You look so serious. Don't worry; it won't bite you. You can try it on but be careful of your nose; might be a little too big." I hold the mask up to my face and make a few moves, trying to bring it to life. Paul says, "You Californians, you're really talented." I do a few more moves, they both laugh and William asks, "How did you become a clown? Is there a school for it?"

I put the mask down. "No, no school. I didn't even want to be a clown; clowns are not cool. I was a juggler, so I was cool."

Paul asks, "Do they teach juggling for PE in San Francisco?"

"No, I learned at a Renaissance Faire."

Paul and William both look puzzled. "It's a big fair where everyone dresses up like they are in Elizabethan England. I had tights, fake velvet bloomers, a tunic and a flat hat with a big feather." Paul says, "Sounds like you were a clown."

"No, man, that was street wear for the kids who ran the games booths. Trust me, we were cool. One of the guys I worked with learned to juggle three croquet balls and he showed me. I started on a Friday and could do a bunch of tricks by the time I got home Sunday night — under the leg, over the top, columns. But I couldn't stand still while I juggled, had to keep walking around. My mom was impressed until I accidently broke a lamp she'd had made. My balls and I were banished to the backyard."

William asks, "Was your mom a circus performer?"

"No, my mom's a sociologist, my dad was a physicist, and my brother is a math genius. Juggling was the first thing I could do that none of them could do better. I loved it. I used to juggle six hours a day."

Paul says, "That's cool."

Paul and William are laughing and listening so intently that I'm tempted to keep telling stories. Luckily, I catch myself and pick up the mask. "Tell me about this. What is the character? Does it have a name?"

Paul looks at William, who shrugs. "Don't know about a name but there is a story that I think goes with this mask." He talks quietly with William in Yup'ik and then turns to me apologetically, "Some of the old stories are private, just for Eskimos, but we think this one is OK to tell you." I say I'd love to hear it.

William sits down on the edge of the desk and starts the story in a soft slightly singsong voice.

> "Once there was an Eskimo man from Eek who traveled to Bethel by dogsled with a white man. They came to an abandoned fish camp and brought their things into one of the old houses. The white man wanted tea but there was no kettle. He had seen pots and kettles in a graveyard near the fish camp but the Eskimo told him not to get anything from the graves. The white man went out anyway and found a kettle to make tea."

Paul interrupts, "You *gussaks* always gotta have your tea." I laugh a little, wondering if the story dated back to when Alaska was Russian. Paul says, "It's OK about the tea because it gives the story dramatic conflict."

William goes on.

> "Anyway, the kettle had small bird eggs in it, which the white guy dumped out. He put snow in the kettle and went into the house to boil the snow to make tea. The Eskimo didn't want any tea.
>
> "As the Eskimo was eating and the white man was drinking his tea, the house started shaking and a fog started coming around the door. The Eskimo said it was a ghost."

"We believe in ghosts, you know. Ghosts are really good for dramatic conflict." Paul stands up. "This is the exciting part."

> "So the fog went whirling up toward the ceiling and the ghost came in under the door. The white man screamed and ran around trying to get out. The Eskimo went right over to the ghost…"

Paul starts playing the Eskimo, making me the ghost. "You see, this is what we are taught to do to ghosts when we're kids."

> "…and he put his hand on the ghost's neck. It felt cold like the ashes from a burned wood fire. He put his other hand on the ghost's head and the ghost started going down under the ground, disappearing."

Paul helps me up from the floor and we sit on the little chairs as William finishes the story.

> "The men ran out of the house and onto their dogsled. They hadn't traveled far when the white man looked back over his shoulder and saw the ghost following them. The Eskimo stopped, took out his knife and put marks in the snow crossing their path. He got back on the sled and called for the dogs to run. The ghost got to those knife marks and slowly sank into the ground.
> "Both men started to feel sick even before they got to Bethel. By the time they made it to the preacher's house, they were both very sick. The preacher made some tea, which made them even sicker.
> "The next morning, the white man and the Eskimo woke up feeling fine but they were still scared. They spent the whole day looking out for ghosts."

Paul gets up and holds the mask, "That story is a little esoteric, isn't it? Birds eggs in the white guy's tea kettle — is that some kind of symbol? Graves and ghosts, an Eskimo who saves the day and a priest who makes you sick. What's all that about? And this mask, is it half Eskimo and half white?" I see a twinkle in Paul's eye and keep quiet. William says, "Paul,

I'm kind of a simple guy so that story always seemed straightforward to me — the white man doesn't understand how we live up here, he doesn't listen to the Eskimo and everyone gets sick." William looks at me, holds up his hands and adds, "Like I said, I'm just a simple guy." I wonder how many times these two have done this routine.

"Well, I'm an artist from California so I can tell you what this story is really about — the white guy planned it all to give the poor Eskimo dude a chance to show off his ninja ghost skills. Simple. It's all about the white guy." Silence, then they explode with laughter. We laugh and snort and laugh louder.

Paul chokes out, "You're funny, man. No wonder you're a clown." We finish laughing and sit quietly on the kindergarten-sized chairs. We sit for a long time. Finally, William asks, "How did you get to know Tina?"

"When I was coming up as a performer, Tina was one of the best clowns in San Francisco — she's older than me…"

"I'm not that much older than you!"

I whip my head around to see Tina standing at the door with her head cocked and her hands on her hips. Her bare legs are sticking out from under my parka.

William stands up, "Hello Tina. If you and Robin are done talking, I'd better be getting home."

Paul follows him to the door, "I'll walk you out. Tomorrow's Monday so I've got to be back here early. See you two in the morning." He winks at me before walking into the hall.

Tina waves as they leave. "That was nice that you called me the best clown in San Fran." I decide not to correct her by mentioning that I said "*one* of the best." She walks over to plant a big kiss on my mouth. "You're not so bad yourself." The parka slides off her shoulders again.

An hour later, we put the chairs back around the little tables, place the books and papers back on the desk and turn off the light as we head to the gym to go to bed.

CHAPTER TEN

WHAT'S IN A NAME
Eek

WAY TOO SOON, TINA AND I are back in Paul Paul's kindergarten class to start our week in Eek. We're both pretty tired but I'm the morning guy and I have an idea. I ask the kids if they know any stories. Right away, they tell us Goldilocks and Red Riding Hood. Disappointed, I ask Paul to tell them the story from last night. He smiles and asks the kids if they want to hear a ghost story. Fifteen sets of eyebrows shoot up.

We've learned, after some awkward moments, that raised eyebrows means "yes." There is a whole nonverbal language out here on the tundra, from slapping one hand, palm down, on your other hand, flipping it quickly and slapping the back side ("he flipped a snowmobile") to elaborate stories drawn with a stick in the snow.

"Are you sure you want a story?" The kids wiggle their eyebrows, saying "yeeeees!!" without saying a word. Paul tells a story in Yup'ik, which I assume is about the Eskimo and the white man who wants tea. After a few minutes, he stands up and switches to English, "So now, do you know what to do when you see a ghost?" Eyebrows shoot up. Tina and I look at each other, silently agreeing that stories would now be part of the day's curriculum.

In our next class, first graders with a teacher from El Paso, we again ask the kids for stories and again get Goldilocks and Red Riding Hood. I notice that John McGinty, the janitor, has slipped in and is sitting near the door. He looks like a taller, older version of William, folding his long frame into a tiny chair. Remembering his position in the village, I ask, "Mr. McGinty, do you know some traditional stories?" The janitor nods his head and waves his hand, inviting the kids to come to him. In a flash, the entire first grade of Eek is cross-legged on the floor in a semicircle around John McGinty. The teacher, a large woman in her 40s wearing wingtip glasses, looks over but goes right back to her reading.

John McGinty speaks in Yup'ik, leaving long pauses that engulf the room in silence. I'm amazed at how still and quiet these first graders are. One pause lasts a full minute and when John starts talking again, he's speaking in English. "So if you meet a *Qamulek*, block his path. The *Qamulek* will ask you, 'What are you doing in my path?' Don't answer the *Qamulek*. You understand?" Eyebrows up. "If you don't answer the question, he will name gifts: a long life, riches, wisdom beyond all wisdom, to be a great hunter. When he says the gift you want, you say, 'Yeah, that's the one I want.' Got it?" John pauses, little eyebrows shoot up. "Then you need to leave the *Qamulek* and never look back. If you do that, you will enjoy your gift until you die."

John McGinty comes to the rest of our morning classes and tells stories in each one. The students are all as rapt as the first graders. Tina and I don't teach much circus but we get a mother lode of material for our show on Friday.

At lunch, we find ourselves waiting in line with a swarm of middle school kids, trying to learn names. One tall, lanky girl is Kennedy, named for JFK. Easy to remember. But one of the kids calls her something else, in Yup'ik. We ask and the kids laugh. They tell us that everyone had a lot of different names — what their cousins call them, what their grandparents call them, nicknames and special Yup'ik names that outsiders should never hear.

We are right in the middle of these kids' lives, living in their school, eating lousy lunches with them, holding them in their cartwheels and performing for their families. We've heard their traditional stories, even if we didn't understand the Yup'ik, but we are only on a first name basis. Kennedy. Their second name is too hard to pronounce and their fourth and fifth names are only for family. Their tenth name is a secret.

THAT EVENING, TINA AND I do a nice show, much better than the last one mostly because I can now use my left arm. After everyone goes home, we pack up and lay out our sleeping bags on a couple of blue three-fold mats in a corner of the gym. We each get in our own bag without saying anything. It's a night for sleeping. Tina scoots over and I put my arm around her. She says, "Good night. I'm beat. You've been hell on my beauty sleep." She gives me a little kiss and rolls over. I roll over with her but my sleeping bag binds around my waist. I struggle to straighten it out. "What are you doing in there, or shouldn't I ask?"

"I'm trying to kiss you good night but my sleeping bag is protecting your virtue."

"Your sleeping bag is very gallant."

I get untangled, kiss Tina on the ear and say, "Good night."

"Good night."

I lie there listening to Tina's breathing and feeling the day drain out of my muscles. My mind is too full to sleep. I wonder about Kennedy's other names. Is she a different girl when she's using one of her secret names? Is "Kennedy" the mask she wears to get through a day of school? To get through a day with us?

Names are important. The kids want to know about my mother's name and all about my father and my brother and why I don't have a sister. "What are their names?" "What do *you* call them?" "Why don't you call your mother 'mom?'" "How did your father die?" They get very close, right up in my lap, too close for comfort.

"John McGinty is pretty amazing." Tina doesn't move and her voice is soft and husky.

My mind reels back into the room as I hear myself say, "Yeah. His stories are gonna be gold for the kids' show."

"He'd be a good father-in-law. I can see why Robin moved here. William's a great guy and those eyes, whew." She quickly adds, "Not as 'whew' as your eyes, of course, but you've got to admit William's got sexy eyes."

I don't admit anything but say, "OK" to cover a flash of jealousy. Tina doesn't notice.

"But it would drive me stark raving mad to live out here in the middle of the frozen tundra, with 200 of my closest relatives."

I chuckle and we're quiet for a few moments.

"My family reunions are bigger than this village — Irish and Italian Catholic, no birth control, lots of kids. I can barely stand them for a couple of days, much less a lifetime…on ice. All they want to know is when I'm getting married." Tina switches to an over-the-top Italian accent, "'You're such a pretty girl but that won't last forever; why don't you settle down and start a family instead of running around with carnies?'" Tina's laugh has a lot of acid in it. "If they only knew I was running around with *Jewish* carnies."

"Jewish *carnies*, plural? Is there someone I don't know about?"

"No, no, you are my only Jewish carney. Promise."

She cranes her neck to give me a kiss and we're quiet again. The heater kicks in. I whisper, "Good night." Tina doesn't say anything. Her breathing is deep and rhythmic. I slowly slide my arm out from under her and roll over.

My family doesn't have reunions. We keep our distance. We like our own space. I like my own space. Even now, after just two days, I'm happy there's a little bit of mat between Tina and me. And the Eskimo kids, cute as they are, are starting to drive me crazy. They want to touch everything and know everything about me but they have secrets they don't tell.

I have secrets, too. I don't tell anyone that my father checked himself out of Bellevue Hospital after a month-long stint, drove our red VW van way out into the Long Island woods, put a rifle in his mouth and fired. I don't tell them that my mother sat on my bed the next morning and told me Daddy was dead, that he'd been sick and killed himself and then offered me the choice of going to school or not that day. I don't want to tell them I went to school and, a year later, when my brother said something about Daddy killing himself, I screamed and screamed at my mother for not telling me. I won't tell them that in the weeks after my father died, I learned that I could end any argument, and get soft-eyed looks, just by mentioning him — but if I added that he'd killed himself, their eyes would harden up and they'd find a way to leave me.

CHAPTER ELEVEN

FIRE AND ICE
Eek

"YOU CALIFORNIANS, you are so tough."

It's Tuesday afternoon. Paul Paul and I are walking in the dark heading for a *maqivik* on the far side of Eek. I've just told him the story of the sauna I took in back in Bethel.

"You jumped right into the snow?"

"Yep." I'm glad he's impressed. He shakes his head and whistles through his teeth, "You're tough."

Right after we finished teaching today, Paul invited me to take a steam bath with the village men.

"These guys are old so don't show off too much." He tells me the names of some of the men who might be there; I repeat them out loud but know they'll fly out of my head before I can use them again. "They don't speak English but don't worry, they'll like you. You're from California."

This is my first real Eskimo experience, the first time I've been invited somewhere that is not in the school or a teacher's house. Tina goes shopping for local crafts in every village, visiting women who make earrings, pins and *yuuyuuks,* what everyone calls Eskimo yo-yos. She always invites me to come with her but I plead poverty. I am saving up for theater school. If I'm honest with myself, I also dread the thought of sitting in a stranger's house and negotiating a price for their artwork. I know that selling crafts is one way that they can make a living without moving to Bethel or Fairbanks, but it feels exploitative. Tina always comes back from these visits bubbling with stories, lists of artists in other villages and little tchotchkes that I have to admit are beautiful.

I want to do more than buy a few souvenirs. We're here as artists; I want to make art, not buy art. Seeing the masks in Paul Paul's classroom, hearing the story about the ghost and then listening to John McGinty telling traditional tales gives me hope. We might get to know the real world of Eek, not just the *gussak* world. And maybe Tina and I can use our art to build bridges between the worlds.

Paul says, "It's getting a little cold. You might not want to jump in the snow tonight."

"I won't."

"Good. You're learning. With all the stories you heard yesterday and now a real Eskimo sauna today, you're almost a native." He turns and winks at me. "Not too much farther; it's just over there by the river."

Yesterday, when we got to the higher grades, the kids started to tell traditional stories themselves. Before speaking, each student would flash a look at John McGinty. I never saw a reaction from the janitor but the students must have seen something because each kid would either start talking or get very quiet. Some old stories are private and Mr. McGinty will let you know if you're about to tell the wrong one.

By the time we got to the high schoolers, we were asking them to act out the stories — one kid sitting on another's shoulders to become a monster, peacock feathers as harpoons, swaying on the rolla bolla board to signify a boat on water. Our show on Friday will be a lot different than anything we've done so far.

"This is the men's *maqivik*."

We're standing in front of A wooden house that's about half the size of the other houses in the village. Paul opens a small door and we walk into the changing room. In the murky light, I see three skinny old men slowly undressing, folding their clothes on the rough wooden benches that line three walls. Paul introduces me in Yup'ik and the trio smiles. They have about 10 teeth between them. I shake hands with each man in turn, being careful to use the village style of one sharp chop down, which they find amusing. They go back to undressing so I start taking off my coat and shoes. Paul hands me a black knit cap that's seen better days. "You'll want to wear this. Keep your hair from catching on fire." I laugh but take the cap. "Have a good steam," and Paul Paul is out the door.

"You're not staying for the..." The door is closed and the old men are naked now with the exception of a wool cap on each of their heads. Their ropy muscles are outlined on their thin bodies. I notice their straight black pubic hair and they catch me staring, which they find hilarious. They turn to go into the second room, the steam room, and I see that their slightly hunched shoulders are covered with red starbursts the size of silver dollars. Stephanie told us that most of the old folks in the villages have perfectly round scars from years of steam baths so hot they explode capillaries. They call them "stamps."

I rush to get naked and duck through the low door into the steam room, holding my knit cap in my hand. I almost walk right into half of a 55-gallon drum turned on its side with a metal tray full of red-hot rocks on top of it. The old guys laugh again — I'm funnier here than on stage — and gesture for me to join them up on the wooden shelf that takes up the half of the room across from the stove. There is barely enough headroom for me to sit cross-legged and it's a lot hotter up here; heat rises. It's definitely hotter than Stephanie's sauna, but I think I can stand it long enough to not look like a wimp. I'm from California. I'm tough.

We sit for a few minutes, sweat pouring out of me and puddling on the plywood shelf. The trio unabashedly examines my body, talking and laughing. I smile, flex my arm muscles and they howl. I'm killing it in the hottest club in Eek.

I figure I can make it another five minutes, maybe six.

One guy hands me a small plastic pail with a little water and a washcloth on the bottom. I wipe my face and feel better. The others put their pails near at hand. The man closest to the hot rocks adjusts his knit cap, takes the washcloth out of his pail and throws the water on the rocks.

I'm on fire.

I'm in a pizza oven. My hair is burning. I slap the cap on my head. I can't breathe. I put the wet washcloth over my mouth. It doesn't help. My hair is on fire under the cap. My capillaries are exploding.

I'm in a fetal position, mouth practically on the plywood. My body is thinking for itself, bypassing my mind. I'm jumping off the shelf, stumbling back through the door into the changing room and slamming the door on the inferno.

I lie on the floor gasping for breath. I rip off my cap to see if my hair is still there.

It is.

I hear muffled Yup'ik and laughter through the door.

I lie there.

Slowly, I pull myself onto the bench, panting. Once my body calms down a little, I start to cycle through emotions — shame at being such a wimpy *gussak*, anger at Paul Paul for setting me up, fear of the heat and finally awe that the old guys are still in that oven. I hear a loud hiss and the changing room gets warmer — another pail of water on the rocks.

I try to convince myself to go back in. "It was the shock of the heat, not the heat itself. Now that I know what it feels like, I'll be ready for it."

Not a chance.

I sit, naked. When my pulse rate is close to normal, I decide to go back to the school before the old guys come out; I don't think I can take another round of ribbing. I see my coat, hat, gloves and boots on the floor near the door; the rest of my clothes are in a pile on the bench. I go to pick them up but they are a frozen mass solidly attached to the external wall.

I look around and see three sets of clothes carefully placed against the internal wall, soaking up the heat from the sauna.

It takes me five minutes to chip my jeans, flannel shirt, socks and boxers off the wall and then another five minutes to thaw the mound of clothing enough to separate out each garment. Getting them on my body is a clown act, a very cold clown act. I finally slide on my boots, grab my coat and walk stiff-legged to the door and out into the arctic night.

Three naked old men can't stop laughing. They're having trouble catching their breath. Whenever they start to calm down, one of them imitates the little whimpering sounds the big *gussak* made as he stumbled out of the *maqivik* and all three of them are off on another round of laughing and wheezing.

Finally one of them manages to splash some water from his bucket onto the rocks. The sauna clouds up, the men duck their heads, exposing their shoulders to the searing steam. They get quiet. They calm down. This is what they love.

They did what Paul Paul asked, invited the *gussak* into the *maqivik*. It is not their fault that the big white man ran out on the first steam. Now they are alone, the three of them, and they can return to the ritual they've done since they were young.

After a long while, one old man slides off the raised plywood platform and through the door to the changing room. The others follow. The *gussak* is gone. The three men dress in silence, as usual. As they are pulling on their boots, one of them asks, "Why did he come to the *maqivik* if he hates steam?"

"He is trying on an Eskimo skin, like you try on a new parka."

"Maybe he should stick to his old parka."

They start laughing again.

CHAPTER TWELVE

YUP'IK CIRCUS
Eek

"…FRIDAY AT SIX IN THE AM, time for Trapline Chatter: First one goes out to Allene in Eek: 'Sold most of the earrings, staying in Fairbanks one more day to try to cash the check, be home tomorrow or for church Sunday; from Mary.' This one's for Father Dan in Bethel…"

I pull the plug out of the wall and the clock radio goes black. Tina mumbles something but settles back in the pillow. Good. She needs her sleep — it's going to be a long day of teaching, rehearsing, getting the kids into makeup and then doing the kids show tonight. We're both squeezed into my sleeping bag so I lie very still.

After surviving the *maqivik* on Tuesday night, the rest of the week has been sweet — classes are going well and we've had something like a social life. Robin invited us over a couple of times, Paul Paul, who I have forgiven, stays after school and visits every day and John McGinty sometimes joins us. We are part of the neighborhood.

Tina and I are in a homey routine, working, eating and sleeping together, stealing kisses and holding hands, doing little favors for each other. I make breakfast every day, "spam du jour" — spam omelets (with powdered eggs), spam hash, fried spam — all served up with pilot bread sporting peanut butter eyes and jam mouths. We sip our tea and eat breakfast sitting on tiny chairs in Paul Paul's room with a tablecloth (clean dishtowel) over a little table. Robin gave us a bottle of Martinelli's sparkling apple juice, which Tina's been serving every evening in champagne flutes (plugged kitchen funnels). Very romantic. Yesterday she bought me an Eskimo yo-yo made of sealskin and beads from Robin's sister-in-law. It's beautiful and I'm getting pretty good at it.

I prepped breakfast before we went to bed last night — powdered eggs, bread, sliced spam, peanut butter, jam — so I can loll around for another 15 minutes. The student show is ambitious, maybe too ambitious. Up until now, we've kept it simple: the kids do a little juggling, some acrobatics, a few clown gags and lots of balancing on stilts and rolla bollas; a basic act-to-act circus, something that Tina and I could put together in any school in any town in America.

This formula worked for the first tentative show in Akiachak, and then for the "big city" kids in Bethel. It worked for the show with our superstar unicyclist George in Kwethluk, and, to a lesser degree, when we did our wounded circus in Kipnuk. Today we're going to try to make something new, something that belongs out here on the tundra, something we could only do in a village — a Yup'ik circus. The performers will have *kusbuks* for costumes, they'll act out Yup'ik stories and their faces will be painted in the style of Paul Paul's masks.

Will the kids remember to ask their grandparents for costumes? Will they be able to do their tricks in *kusbuks*? Will John McGinty nix one of the stories at the last minute, making us cut a whole class from the show? What if one of the other old folks objects to a story? Or to our whole show? Will they stand up and walk out? Yell at us? Tell us to go home?

I carefully shimmy out of the sleeping bag before I follow this train of thought too far. I pull on some pants, head to the kitchen and start dipping bread in the egg mixture. Yesterday I asked the basketball kids to take the morning off — hopefully they'll remember so Tina and I can eat a leisurely breakfast before our 8 am class. I get two pans going, spam and French toast, and make pilot bread faces until it is time to put breakfast on hold and wake up Tina. Even with kisses and cuddles, she's a bear in the morning.

Someone is dribbling a basketball. Damn. Sometimes these kids…

After making sure that Tina is out of bed, I walk into to the gym to negotiate with the basketball players. There is just one girl, standing on the foul line holding a ball under her arm. Molly McGinty, John's youngest daughter, Chuna's baby sister. Molly's a senior, a big, tall girl who hasn't said a word, or done much of anything, all week. "I'm not doing the show tonight." Her voice is soft and her village accent is thick. I wait a moment, thinking she'll go on, and finally say, "Oh. That's too bad."

She shoots and the basketball flies off the rim right at me. I catch it and throw a bounce pass back to Molly. She shoots again, a little short, and the ball pops up off the front of the rim. I rebound and then get an idea. "I'll make you a deal. Let's play one-on-one. I win, you do the show; if you win, you sit it out." Molly smiles and her face is radiant for a second before she drops back to her habitual scowl. "Deal. Half court, play to 21, win by two, clear every possession and call your own fouls." She rockets a two-handed pass into my chest. "You take it out."

I've got at least four inches and 50 pounds on her so all I need to do is work in under the basket for layups and then play her tight on defense. I dribble in from half court; she plays off me until I get to the top of the key and then quickly goes for a steal. I dart around to my left — being a juggler helps me drive with either hand — and I'm clear to the basket. But on my next dribble the ball hits a frost heave and flies out of bounds.

Her ball.

She takes it out at half court, dribbles in about 10 feet and launches a jump shot. Swish. Damn, have to play her tight all the way out. She takes it in again, I'm on her with my arms out, left hand swiping at the ball and then she's past me. Layup. Two to zip.

Ten minutes later it's over. 21 — 2. She didn't miss a shot. I'm standing mid-court, bent over at the waist with my hands on my knees dripping sweat on the hardwood. Tina, who must have been watching for a while, claps loudly and comes over to give Molly a high-five. "You can play, girl!"

"Thanks." Molly carefully puts the ball down on the foul line and walks out of the gym.

When I catch my breath, I say, "We just lost a performer for the show tonight" with a little more venom than I had intended.

"Did you bet the show on that game?"

"It seemed like a good way to get Molly engaged."

Tina laughs, "She was engaged alright, engaged enough to kick your ass." I shoot Tina a look. She adds, "No big loss, she was only going to hand props and stand in the back of the big scarf juggling act. Beating you in b-ball was her show. We'll be fine without her tonight."

I don't say anything. "You OK? You were working your bad arm pretty hard." I realize that my elbow is throbbing but I don't think I've done any real harm. On the other hand, it is a good way to save face. "It's not too bad but I could use some ice." A worried look flashes across Tina's face and she hurries into the kitchen. Over her shoulder she yells, "If you reinjure that arm, I'll kick your ass. And you know I can."

There is ice in the freezer, which Tina brings back in a plastic bag. "You've had a tough time here in Eek — the old guys try to broil you and now Molly McGinty cleans your clock in b-ball." I walk away from her and sit down on pile of mats, leaning against a wall of the gym to nurse my elbow. She walks out of the gym.

A few minutes later, Tina hands me a plate of French toast with spam and sits down next to me with a plate of her own. "You don't need to get all huffy." We chew and stare at the floor. After a few minutes, she says, "I'm worried about the show tonight, especially the acrobatics. All the storytelling and the extra rehearsals really cut into our training time."

My elbow is numb, a high school girl just beat me one-on-one and now Tina's attacking my theatrical ideas.

"The stories *are* the show. That's what we're doing here. Without the stories, we're as bad as 'Dallas' on TV or the racist teachers from Texas."

"Whoa, easy. I've got nothing against your precious stories and I sure wasn't saying anything racist about the kids. Remember, I'm the one who booked this gig; I'm the one who got us out here in Eskimo country."

She takes a deep breath and I smartly keep my mouth shut.

"All I am saying is that the big pyramid the sophomores are doing is pretty shaky. It doesn't matter how much we celebrate Yup'ik culture if we hurt a bunch of their children."

We're quiet again and before either of us can say anything a gang of middle schoolers races into the gym. They're playing full court before they even notice us.

Tina looks at her watch, "We've got 15 minutes 'til we've gotta rehearse with Paul Paul's kids."

IN THE SHOW, WE DON'T HURT ANY KIDS but I'm not sure if we do them any favors, either. It's a mess — carefully painted mask designs half sweated off of little faces, feet slipping on *kusbuk* fringes when kids try to do pyramids and stories told in tiny voices that even the other performers can't hear. Tina was right that some of the acrobatic tricks are dangerously under-trained and all the time we put into acting out the stories doesn't seem to make a difference; they looked as rough and raw as they had earlier in the week.

But the crowd loves it. They clap so long that the kids have re-do most of their acts three or four times. The gym is full for a couple of hours after the show and kids are coming up to introduce us to their whole families. When grandparents start talking to us in Yup'ik, kids step in to translate.

Molly McGinty half-smiles when she introduces Tina and me to her great aunt Allene, Agnes McGinty's sister. Allene is a tiny woman with a babushka over her gray hair and a bright blue-and-orange *kusbuk*. Almost chanting in Yup'ik, with lots of hissing sounds as she blows air through the gaps between her teeth, Allene tells us a different ending for one of the stories we used in the show, a romantic legend about a seal hunter who marries the Spirit of the Island. Molly translates in a soft monotone.

> "After the Spirit of the Island got pregnant, her husband went away and didn't come back. The Spirit of the Island gave birth on her own. Then she took her baby and searched for nights and days until she found her husband in the hut of another woman."

I'm pretty sure John McGinty didn't tell the fourth graders this part.

> "The Spirit of the Island stood outside of this hut and sang of her sorrow and pain and as she did, the roof caved in and crushed her unfaithful husband."

Allene's voice gets louder and Molly echoes her great aunt.

> "On her way home, the Spirit of the Island stopped in the little village of Eek, where she met a really cute

young man, half her age, and they got married."

By the time Allene finishes, a dozen old women are standing around us. They laugh so loudly I can barely hear Molly's translation. Tina is laughing with the women and Allene opens her arms for a hug. Tina squeezes her tight and I hear the old woman say, in English, "You got a young one, too" and then switches back to Yup'ik. Molly quickly comes over to translate; "Now you know what to do if he ever leaves you."

"I LOVE THOSE WOMEN!" Tina is wrapping the burlap on the ends of the bundles of stilts while I heat up some leftover mac and cheese for dinner. "The stories *after* the show were better than the ones *in* the show." I'd love to argue but I just keep stirring.

CHAPTER THIRTEEN

SHOTS FIRED
Mountain Village

"HOW'S THE ELBOW, CLOWN BOY?" Without waiting for an answer, Jenny puts her arms behind her head, leans back and closes her eyes. I'm a little slow to grab the yoke, which I've learned is the proper name for an airplane steering wheel, so Tina smacks me on the shoulder from the back seat. "Don't mess around — I hate these planes!" I give her a thumbs-up and take a quick look at the control panel.

Jenny says, "We got a long trip, Clown Girl. Mountain Village is all the way up on the Yukon so settle in. Clown Boy'll just keep her going due north for 30 minutes and then wake me up." I'm pretty sure Jenny's not actually planning on taking a nap but Tina is staring holes into the side of my head. I check the control panel again, this time registering our altitude, speed and direction, which is due north. Keep everything steady for half an hour and we'll be fine.

Tina yells over the roar of the engine, "Hey, Jenny, want to see the *uluaq* I bought from Mary Carter yesterday in Eek?" I'm sure Tina is more worried that Jenny might be napping than she is interested in showing off her latest purchase. Jenny doesn't move, "I've seen too many Yup'ik trinkets in my time."

"No, check it out. This is a real one. It has a walrus ivory handle."

Tina hands Jenny the knife, which has a cardboard sheath over its half-moon steel blade. Jenny feels the handle and opens her eyes. For the next 20 minutes the two women talk about the quality of the knife (high), chopping techniques, and how a Yup'ik *uluaq* is different from an Aleut *ulu* and *ulus* from Canada, Siberia and Greenland. Who knew?

They'll talk, I'll fly and we'll all get to Mountain Village alive.

When Jenny sees the frozen Yukon River snaking across the tundra 500 feet below us, she takes her yoke and banks the Cessna to the left, heading downriver toward the Bering Sea. I'm relieved, especially since the skies are turning cloudy and the wind is bouncing the little plane. "Nice flying, Clown Boy. I'll take her into Mountain Village. I'd let you land but there's a bit too much weather coming up." Jenny pats my knee, Tina puts her knife back in her bag and I exhale.

About 15 minutes later, we see a village on the north side of the Yukon river and Jenny gets the plane lined up to land. "We got company." Jenny points to another plane sitting on the side of the landing strip. A man, who I assume is the pilot, is looking up at us and waving his arms. "We'll land first and then they'll take off. Stay in the plane after we land so you don't get tangled up in their prop. Had a guy once…" Tina finishes Jenny's sentence, "…who slid into the prop. You've told us. Hamburger." Jenny beams, "You know my stories, Clown Girl! I'm flattered."

We glide to a stop at the end of the strip and I look out the window at the other plane, a bright yellow single prop with brown accents. Jenny says, "Oh, hell yeah, a de Havilland Beaver. Love those planes! Don't make 'em any more but man, do they fly nice! Tough little fuckers, too." The other pilot waves from the cockpit as he starts to take off and I get a peek at a *gussak* couple in the back seats staring straight ahead.

We unload, Jenny takes off and I see the lights of the school down a small hill a few hundred yards away. It's started to snow and the wind is whipping the flakes so hard they seem to be flying up instead of down.

The door to the school is unlocked, even though it's Sunday, and we walk down the long, neon-lit hall. On a half-opened door we see a simple metal sign "Principal." We go in and stand in front of a bald man in an off-white shirt, head down over his desk, writing. Without looking up he says, "Kinda busy here. Can we talk in the morning?"

The nameplate on the desk says "Dr. Smith." I feel like I did as a kid, standing in the principal's office after being sent out of class for making some lame joke.

After a few moments, Tina says, "We're the artists in residence, the circus program." Dr. Smith looks up. He's wearing a red bow tie. "I cancelled that program. Got too much going on. We can't have you at the school right now." He starts writing again. We don't say anything so he looks back up and slowly explains, "Go down to the store, use the phone to call Stephanie and get a charter back to Bethel." I turn to walk out the door but Tina stops me. "We were just in Bethel, with Stephanie, and she sent us here. Clearly she doesn't think the program is cancelled."

Dr. Smith slams down his pen, "Damn it, would you leave me alone! Two of my best teachers just flew out of here, I've got a ninth-grader who could to be arrested for attempted murder and the fucking missionaries are trying to start a civil war. Pardon my French." Tina and I are too stunned to move. We must have looked shocked because, after taking a breath, Dr. Smith stands up and says, "I'm sorry. Bad day."

We introduce ourselves, shake hands village style, and Dr. Smith invites us to sit down. "Here's how it is: Friday afternoon a boy put a couple of bullets through a window over in teachers' housing. No one got hurt but it scared the couple who lived there right back to Texas." He adds, "She's pregnant," as if he needs to explain why people would leave Alaska just because they've been shot at.

"My best teachers and the only ones who were here to teach instead of save souls. The kicker is the kid got the wrong house — he was gunning for someone else, a single guy who couldn't teach his way out of a paper bag. So now I'm stuck with a trigger-happy freshman *and* the teacher he's trying to kill; everybody's taking sides and I'm going to be in the classroom myself until the district gets me a couple of subs, who don't want to come because they're scared to get shot at. And now you two are here to make a fucking circus. Pardon my French."

Dr. Smith eventually agrees to let us stay the night. "I'll tell you in the morning if you can be here all week." Right before we walk out, he adds, "But even if you stay, you cannot physically be in the building from 8 am to 3 pm; after school only." He dismisses us with a little wave. "Now, please, I've got to finish these incident reports and teacher requests."

CHAPTER FOURTEEN

ALARM BELLS
Mountain Village

TINA AND I FIND A SLED and hand-pull our equipment down from the landing strip. By the time we get back to the school, the principal is gone. We load our bags and stilts into a closet, scrounge up some PBJ on pilot bread and roll out our sleeping bags on a couple of blue mats in a corner of the gym. We try to practice our juggling act with all four hands, but our hearts aren't in it. We zip our sleeping bags together, cuddle in and start to figure out what we'll do if we stay — Where will we go during the days? Will anyone want to do circus skills in the midst of a civil war? Will the kid try to shoot the other teacher, the one he was trying to kill in the first place?

Tina is seriously pissed at Dr. Smith. "This sucks. We're here to teach, in school, during the day, not after school. He has a responsibility to let us do our work. And if he doesn't, there's no way I'm hanging around in Bethel all week. If this village goes south, I'm going home." I'm mad too, but more concerned about losing two weeks' pay and cutting short my tundra romance with Tina. Even if we stay together back in San Francisco, it won't be the same as it is up here in Alaska.

I try to smooth things over, which only gets Tina more pissed off. Finally, she gets up, turns off the gym lights, slides back on her side of the "bed" and says, "Wake me up a 6:30 — no way I'm talking to Doctor Fucking Smith without some caffeine in me." We fall asleep without a goodnight kiss.

I'm dreaming I'm late for class. The bell is ringing

and I can't find the right room. It's dark, I can't find the door. "What the fuck?" It's Tina, screaming.

I'm awake. It's dark and the bell is ringing.

"What the fuck? The school bell?"

The ringing stops.

Tina says, "Can you believe this place?"

I get up and turn on the lights. The big clock above the basketball hoop says midnight.

"If that thing rings again, I'm going home tomorrow. Period. This is crap."

I try to hug her but she turns away. At 12:05, the bell rings again. Tina curses a blue streak.

The bell stops and it's quiet.

We hear the front door open and we both jump up. A woman in her 30s wearing a fur-lined *kusbuk* over her nightshirt bustles into the gym. "Oh, you *are* here. And the bell is going off. I'm so sorry. I heard the circus people were in town and then I heard the bell go off; we live right across the street. It does that sometimes, starts ringing at midnight as if it's 8 am, something to do with the circuits. I'm so sorry."

Tina says, "It's not your fault" and we introduce ourselves.

"I'm Mary Joshua. My husband Michael is the custodian. I'll go wake him up and he can stop the bells."

Michael Joshua ends up having to up cut some wires to stop the bells, "Don't know what's wrong but I can fix it all tomorrow. At least you'll get some sleep tonight. We're glad you're here — our kids are excited to be in the circus." I'm glad someone's excited.

TINA IS UP THE MINUTE the alarm goes off at 6:30 am; she's dressed and drinking a cup of tea by 6:40. "I'm going down to the store to call Stephanie, tell her to book us flights back to San Francisco today!" She puts on her coat and boots and almost runs over Mary Joshua, who's coming in with a big bowl of hot oatmeal. Mary tells Tina that the store doesn't open until eight and that we can wait at her house after we eat our oatmeal.

We're standing at the counter of the village store, one dimly lit room with shelves half full of odds and ends — potato chips, batteries, Cheerios and Campbell's soup, with vanilla extract and cough syrup behind the counter because they can get you high. Everything costs twice what it would in the bodegas near my apartment. There are two Eskimo women standing near us, eavesdropping while waiting for the phone.

"Stephanie, we're not staying, even if that jerk says we can teach after school." This is the third time Tina's said this and I can tell she's starting to lose her edge.

A few minutes later, Tina hangs up, hands the phone to the next woman in line and walks out of the store. When we're almost to the school, she says, "We're going to stay. There's nothing in our contracts about only teaching during school hours. Stephanie's calling Smith right now, reading him the riot act and making sure he gets us a bed to sleep on in a teacher's house."

Clearly Stephanie is as effective with Dr. Smith as she was with Tina because when we walk into his office, the principal is all smiles, if a little forced. "You can teach from 3 pm to 5 pm in the gym today and do your show at 7 pm tonight. Then you can do three to five all week and have the student show at 6 pm on Friday. How does that sound for a schedule?"

Tina snaps, "Where do we sleep?"

"I've arranged hosts for both of you — a single male teacher and a couple. You can stay at their places during the day and, of course, sleep on their couches." Tina and I look at each other. He misunderstands and adds, "Houses are small up here; we don't have guest rooms." It looks like I'll be missing Tina sooner than I thought, although we will have our days together. I give her a little shrug and Tina turns to Dr. Smith, "We need to eat, too." The principal is clearly relieved, "Yes, of course. These teachers have opened their homes to you and they got extra groceries this morning."

We go off to meet our hosts in their classrooms: I'm with Tim Colbert, a young math teacher from Arizona, and Tina's with Amy and Ernie Wright, both veteran elementary teachers from Austin. They give us directions to their houses. "The doors are unlocked so make yourselves at home."

We walk to the Wright's home first. Tina says, "I'm going to unpack and take a nap. I'll come by your place when I wake up." We kiss and she goes into the house.

I walk into Tim Colbert's house and put my bag down on the floor. It's big for a village house, three rooms with a shabby orange couch that takes up nearly half the living room. I sit on the couch and stare out the large front window. It's quiet. I'm alone and in a house. It's wonderful not to hear the echoes of a gym and to look out a window. Alone. I take a deep breath and feel both exhausted and elated. Tim's house is warm, there's food in the kitchen and I don't have to teach for six hours. Heaven.

After a while I get bored with staring out the window and pick up my murder mystery *J is for Judgment*. Pretty quickly I'm rereading pages so I put the book down, eat a cheese sandwich and lie on the couch.

"GET UP, SLEEPY HEAD. We got some circus to teach." I force open my eyes and look up at Tina, who is leaning over me. My throat is sore and my lids are heavy. "I'm up."

"You look like hell; you OK?"

"Yeah, just groggy; don't usually take naps."

Tina walks into the kitchen and a moment later I smell coffee brewing. "We've got one hour to figure out what we're teaching this afternoon, assuming that anyone shows up. Then we better talk through the show for tonight. We should also start thinking how the hell we're going to get the kids ready for their show on Friday with just 10 hours of class time, total. For the week. No stories, that's for sure. Probably no acrobatics, either."

The coffee helps wake me up but my throat feels like I gargled with a belt sander. Tina does most of the talking in our meeting and then up at the school. Thirty-five kids are there at three o'clock, more than we expected. Most of them stay until five and then hang around to watch us warm up for the show. At 7 pm, there are only about 20 adults in the bleachers, with Mary and Michael Joshua right up front. A couple of dozen more folks trickle in during the show, including all three of our hosts. This is our sparsest crowd all tour and, after our final bow, most of the adults head right for the door.

As usual, the kids surround Tina and me, wanting to play with our props. But when Tim Colbert, my host, comes over, the kids disappear.

Tim and I chat for a few minutes while Tina talks to the Joshuas and the Wrights. A few moments later, she signals me to join them. Tim says, "I'll see you at home. Are you hungry? I've got lots of frozen salmon I can cook up." I thank Tim and go over to Tina. She watches my host leave and then hustles me into the closet where we store our props.

"He's the guy the kid was shooting at!"

"What?"

"Tim, your host, is the teacher the kid meant to shoot."

Mary Joshua is scared. The children are asleep already — they ran around the gym for almost an hour after the circus show — and the house is clean. Michael is still over at the school, locking up after the last people leave. It's quiet in the kitchen.

The shooting scared Mary and then the Watkins flew off; she can't blame them, but Mr. Watkins was her son's teacher and the poor boy cried all day yesterday. Now the circus is here and her kids are happy again but it won't last long — the circus man is staying with Mr. Colbert.

Mr. Colbert is a bad teacher but the Chicklak boy shouldn't have shot at him. Or tried to shoot at him but instead shot out the Watkins' window and scared them away. Forever. What was he thinking? What is wrong with him?

The Chicklak boy is still in town. Sure, they took his rifle away but he can get another one in a second and go shoot up Mr. Colbert's house with the circus man in it. Then the boy would go to jail and this town would never get a decent teacher again. The circus folks certainly won't come back — who wants to teach kids who shoot at you? Who wants to live in a village where kids shoot at teachers?

Mary can't leave Mountain Village. She and Michael don't know anywhere else. Besides, Michael has a good job that keeps him home and safe; no trips up to the oil fields in Prudhoe Bay where men lose arms and legs and women steal husbands. She and Michael will stay and the good *gussaks* will go and Mary will try to keep her kids safe and happy.

CHAPTER FIFTEEN

SHOT IN THE BACK(SIDE)

Mountin Village

THE RED NUMBERS on the alarm clock read 2:12. I'm pretty sure it's the nighttime 2:12, not the afternoon 2:12. My throat is sore, the room is boiling hot and I'm scared. The window I stared out of yesterday is now a real and present danger. I still don't know which ninth grader was the shooter; maybe he was one of the kids who learned to juggle scarves yesterday or hugged me at the end of the show last night. Whoever he is, there is nothing to stop him from shooting through Tim's window and accidently putting a bullet through my head.

4:45 am. I must have dozed off. I'm still alive. Need to drink some water.

6:10 am. No need to wake up early. I'll turn off the alarm. Tim must be getting up soon.

"GOOD MORNING. Or should I say good afternoon." Tina is perched next to me. It's light out. "Time to get up; we teach in an hour. This couch must be some kind of comfy." She leans in to kiss me; I try to talk but a croak comes out and she pulls back. "You OK? You look pasty." She puts her hand on my forehead. "Shit, you are burning up. No way you can teach today with that fever." I say I'm fine but the sound of my voice only seals the deal — I'm a sick puppy.

"It's OK, I'll keep them going with juggling and teach some balancing with feathers, maybe a little tumbling. We can do stilts and rolla bolla tomorrow." Tina makes me some tea with honey and heads off to teach.

I don't know quite how, but I end up on the steps of the village health aide's office. It's twilight. Tim is holding my arm. He opens the door and I walk into the waiting room. The health aide, a thin Eskimo woman in her early twenties wearing a white coat, comes out of her office, looks at my throat and clucks her tongue. "Lots of puss pockets. Might be strep." As a kid I had strep throat at least once a year so I'm sure she's right. She asks if I'm allergic to penicillin. I'm not, and she says she'll give me a shot in a couple of hours, after she sees some other patients.

Tim leads me home; I fall asleep on the couch for a while and then find my way back to the clinic. The health aide calls me into her office and starts to prep the shot. "It needs to be in your rear end. Sorry about that. You can pull down your pants and I'll be ready in a minute."

I'm leaning on the examining table with my bare ass sticking out. It's getting cold so I look over my shoulder to see if she's got the shot ready. Five old women are crammed into the doorway, stifling giggles. They see me seeing them; they burst out laughing and wave cute little waves. The health aide makes some apologetic sounds, shoos the old ladies away and sticks a big needle in my right cheek.

THE PENICILLIN HELPS but I'm weak for days. Tina comes over every morning to make me tea and toast. She reports on how things are going — the kids have taken well to juggling, not so great on unicycle and rolla bolla; The Wrights are good hosts and cook nice food; Dr. Smith hasn't said a word to her; and Mary Joshua comes in every afternoon to help her manage the students. Oh, and the state troopers were here to question the boy about the shooting. Apparently it had to do with religion, like Dr. Smith said, but a civil war is a bit of an exaggeration.

I tell her that I'm still alive and that Tim seems like a nice enough guy except when he asks to pray for me and offers to read to me from the Book of Mormon. Tina makes sympathetic sounds. We sit and look out the window.

I feel guilty as hell, leaving Tina to teach alone, again. Never missing a show is a point of pride for me. Classes are like mini-shows. I'm letting my partner down, I'm weak, I'm not really a pro. To make it worse, I keep wondering when Tina will find out she likes teaching alone better than working with me.

When Tina comes over on Thursday morning, I tell her I'm feeling good enough to teach but she tells me I shouldn't push it, that she's in a rhythm. I want to argue but I don't have the energy. She kisses me on the forehead and says, "It'll all equal out — I'm planning to take a break next week in Emmonak."

I hope she's joking.

7:35 AM FRIDAY. Someone is knocking on the door. Tim's sweatpants walk by at eye level. I roll off the couch and slide into the kitchen — I'm not presentable yet. Cold air blows into the house. Some murmurs float into the kitchen. Tim pokes his head in and says, "I gotta go to Bethel today. If I'm not back before you leave, have a good trip." I say, "Thanks for everything." As the door closes, I get a glimpse of two men in blue uniforms and big hats. I brush my teeth.

A little while later, Tina comes over to warn me that the civil war is heating up. She was at the store when the state troopers arrived in town. Apparently the 14-year-old shooter and his family are in Bethel for questioning; rumor has it that Tim Colbert may not be coming back to Mountain Village and Dr. Smith is going nuts. The boy and his family are Moravian and they say that Tim was trying hard to convert him to Mormonism. The Moravians, about half the town, are furious at Tim for targeting the boy, getting him so freaked out that he resorted to violence. The other side, the Mormons, are furious at the Moravians for talking trash about Tim, which encouraged the kid to shoot at him (or shoot at a house he thought was Tim's).

As Tina's talking, I make some coffee and pour two bowls of Cheerios. We eat and sip for a minute before Tina adds, "Here's the really bad news — folks are saying that you are a Mormon because you've been staying here at Tim's house."

"What?"

"A lot of Moravians aren't letting their kids do the show tonight because you'll be there."

"Did you mention that I'm Jewish?"

"Yep, but they still think you're Mormon. Luckily, the Wrights are Catholic, which is neutral, kind of the Switzerland of Mountain Village religions, so I'm OK. The end result is that only the Mormon and Catholic kids will be at the gym at 3 pm."

THE "SHOW" IS MORE OF an open workshop with about 25 students, watched by their parents. The Joshuas, who are Moravian, buck the boycott and come with their kids, who have fun with the peacock feathers. The Wrights come, of course, but Dr. Smith doesn't bother to show up. We are all done and packed in under an hour. No stories, no acrobatics, no show really.

The stories in Mountain Village are the stuff of tragedy, not circus. After our ambitious "Yup'ik circus" in Eek, even with all its faults, this show was just sad. I should have sucked it up and taught at least a few of the days, we should have pushed Smith for more time with the students and we should have tried to convince the different Christian sects that circus is a demilitarized zone, a place for everyone. We didn't do any of that.

Saturday morning, Jenny flies us to Bethel for a day of R&R. Back at the old hotel, Stephanie gets an earful from Tina about Dr. Smith while I go off to visit Roger Dent at the clinic to make sure the elbow's doing OK and the strep is gone.

That night, lying in a real bed with Tina nestled next to me, 100 miles from Mountain Village, I say, "Thank you for doing all the teaching. Sorry I was such a wimp."

"The teaching was fine, it was everything else that sucked. And I felt bad the kids didn't get to do a real show. Mostly, I got bored."

"Maybe we can do something about that."

She wiggles her eyebrows, "Maybe we can."

After making love, Tina Edgars dozes for a while but is too restless to really sleep. She slips out of bed, pulls on the PJs she'd tossed on the floor and feels her way to the kitchen without turning on a light. In the dark, she finds Stephanie's liquor stashed discreetly behind a huge sack of dog food; on her other visits, Tina had noticed that whenever Stephanie got up to feed the dog, some wine, beer or whiskey would appear on the table when she sat back down.

Tina pours a shot of Black Jack into a coffee cup, sits at the table and drinks the whiskey neat. The house is quiet, a kind of quiet she never hears in San Francisco. The drink makes her sad, and then angry. She came to the bush excited to get swept up in an alien world, an Eskimo world, and she'd almost felt it in Eek, almost touched what Robin touches every day — a life so different from hers it changes you forever. She doesn't want this other life, she just wants to shake up her city self, her California dreaming self, her circus self, jog her lazy way with weather and travel and love. She almost felt it in Eek but then there was Mountain Village. Fucking Mountain Village!

Flushed with anger and Black Jack, she catches herself right before the cup hits the table. Damn those missionaries! Damn Dr. Smith! Damn Tim Colbert. Nothing but small-minded small-town America on a slab of ice. Nothing new, nothing real.

Tina sits for another few minutes and her anger starts to droop. She gets up, feels for the faucet to rinse her cup. The water sounds like Niagara Falls and she quickly turns it off. She stands at the sink, waiting to hear footsteps. None come and she finds her way back to bed.

CHAPTER SIXTEEN

THE MOUTH OF THE YUKON
Emmonak

"LOOK DOWN. YOU SEE THAT 'Y' in the Yukon River?" Jenny is playing tour guide. "One fork goes up to Norton Sound but we're taking the other one, the west fork, heading toward the Bering Sea." In a few minutes we're looking down at the mouth of the Yukon River. Even completely iced over it's impressive — a huge triangular delta opening out to the frozen ocean. Jenny makes a big loop so Tina can get a couple of pictures before landing the Cessna in Emmonak, just a little northeast of the mouth. Our last village.

Stephanie warned us that there are tensions in Emmonak, but the lines are cultural, not religious. Unlike other villages, where the only folks from the lower forty-eight are teachers, Emmonak is the commercial fishing hub of the Yukon coast. It also has a small airport, and both of these operations bring in more *gussaks*.

A couple of teachers meet us planeside on the gravel runway and take us right back to the teachers' complex. They tell us that there's a party every Sunday after church and we're this week's special guests.

The two-bedroom apartment would feel at home in any suburb in America. It is overflowing with people chatting in little groups, eating burgers and chips off of red plastic plates and drinking beer from red plastic cups (apparently it's illegal to sell or import alcohol in Emmonak but there's no law against drinking it). Debby Boone is on the stereo.

We get introduced around and I end up on a couch, surrounded by women. They are all teachers and they are all white. Everyone here is white. The women are asking questions, starting with basics like "How did you become a clown?" and then moving to nosy, like "Are you and Tina married?" and pretty quickly getting down to business:

"Don't go to the kids' homes, even if they invite you. They live like pigs and their houses reek of rancid seal oil."

"Keep everything simple in class; the students here are at least two grade levels behind."

"And that's the smart ones."

"Watch out for those Eskimo women; they are hot for white men. They'll jump your bones like dogs in heat if you give them half a chance."

That's enough for me; once you start talking about "them," and "they" smell and act like animals, you're heading down the same road that led to Anne Frank hiding in an attic.

I make some noises about being tired from the long flight, find Tina and walk out. As we hit the snow, she says, "Damn, I felt like fresh meat in there. Every single man, and a few married ones, hit on me." I tell her about my session with the women teachers. She says, "Why the hell are they up here in Alaska if they think all the students are dumb and their mothers are dogs?" I don't say anything so Tina answers her own question: "Maybe that's just their way of flirting, you know, a little racism to set the hook and then land you with 'dog in heat.'" I chuckle. "I don't think so." "Why not? You're a good catch." She gives me a quick kiss.

I stop, look at her and get sad. I miss her already. I lean down to give her a real kiss and then slowly lift her up. As her feet come off the ground, she wraps her legs around my waist. We stand there in the snow giving the local gossips plenty of material. Tina jumps down and, as we keep walking, she says, "I guess those lady teachers got you warmed up."

We find our gear neatly stacked near the front door of the school. We schlep the circus stuff into a closet in the gym, take our personal gear back over to the teachers' complex and find our apartment; it's a perfect match to the one we just partied in.

"This place is like the set for *I Love Lucy*." She leaves her cold weather gear at the door and starts dancing from bedroom to bedroom singing the *Lucy* theme song with lyrics I didn't even know existed.

"I love Lucy and she loves me. We're as happy as two can be."

She dances over to the kitchen table and mimes eating chocolates and shoving them down her shirt. I laugh — she's damn good. I say "Lu-cy!" in my best Desi Arnaz accent. She opens her eyes wide in Lucy's classic "Who me?" look.

"Sometimes we quarrel but then
How we love making up again."

She runs over to me singing the next verse and fitting the action to the words.

"Lucy kisses like no one can.
I'm yer missus and you're my man."

We do the little soft-shoe duet from our clown act, ending with Tina jumping into my arms. She keeps singing as I carry her into one of the bedrooms.

"And life is heaven you see.
Cause I love Lucy
And she loves me."

We land on the bed.

A WHILE LATER, TINA'S HUNGRY for dessert. I go check the fridge, which is surprisingly well stocked, and bring in two plastic bowls of chocolate ice cream and crushed Oreos. We sit up in bed eating. We're quiet, letting a sweet moment linger.

Tina takes the empty bowls into the kitchen and on the way back says, "There was a guy at the party, a geologist. He was telling me the river is closing up because the crap that gets dumped upriver floats down and makes a dam at the mouth. This other guy, a fisherman, starts on a tirade about how Eskimos put all their trash out on the river ice in winter — honey buckets, broken toys, old snowmobiles — and at break-up it all washes down. The fisherman says, 'They got no respect for the land,' which seemed strange coming from someone who's trying to wipe out the wild salmon run, but I kept my mouth shut. The geologist mumbled something about all the really big stuff that is clogging up the river is made in the lower forty-eight and shipped up here. The other guy called him a pussy. You think about it, though; even two generations ago Eskimos didn't own *anything* that could clog the Yukon. Back then, whatever they dumped on the ice would disintegrate before it got to the next village downriver."

"Humans were specks on the tundra, little vulnerable specks." She props herself on a pillow. "We still are, except now we have snowmobiles and heaters and planes. Little specks with big toys." She starts talking about how weather shapes culture, which, in turn, shapes the artwork and mythology. And she's telling some of the stories she's heard from the craftswomen she met, stories about skinning seals and fish camp and carving walrus tusks. I'm content to listen until the words start to blur and I'm startled awake by an elbow in the ribs, "Wake up and listen to me! You're the one who's all hot for Yup'ik stories."

"Sorry. I love the stories but you wore me out."

Tina snorts, pokes me again and jumps up to go get our stuff that's still sitting by the door. We unpack, get into our PJs, jump back in bed and sleep straight through to the alarm.

CHAPTER SEVENTEEN

SHOT IN THE BACK
Emmonak

IT WAS STRANGE TO HAVE blond and brown-haired kids in most of the classes today. Luckily none of the racism we heard at the party came out of these kids' mouths.

Now it's after school and our "open gym" is packed. Two 13-year-olds, best friends, are the stars: Dougie and Barnsie look like brothers, with Dougie being a little shorter and Barnsie having longer hair. Barnsie is amazing at anything that takes great balance — stilt walking, rolla bolla and unicycle; Dougie's got juggling hands and is passing balls and learning three clubs when we have to end the class to get the room ready for our show. The two friends help us set up and then hang around to talk and get some more coaching.

It's 5:30 pm and Tina says, "Boys, don't you have to get home to dinner?" Two sets of black eyebrows shoot up. "Good, because we need to warm up for our show." Barnsie looks at Dougie, who is a little more outgoing. Dougie looks down at the floor and says, "We want to visit at your house."

Visiting is very popular in Eskimo villages and it can be as simple as going over someone's house, sitting quietly for a few minutes or a few hours, and then leaving. But inviting a couple of 13-year-old boys over for an evening visit sounds like courting trouble, especially in this village.

Tina takes the lead. "Why don't you go home now and ask your parents if it's OK to visit tomorrow night?" Two sets of eyes look at the floor. "Is there something else you want to ask?" Eyebrows shoot up.

"Well…" This time Barnsie gets the courage to say, "We want to have a sleepover at your house."

Now we're on quicksand. Sure, this is our last village and we've got an opportunity to get to know these two boys better than any other kids we've met, know them well enough to remember them years from now. They have great circus skills and work hard…my mind races ahead to helping them get out of Emmonak and onto the international circus circuit. But a sleepover…

Tina says, "Let's take one step at a time. Dougie, Barnsie, we really like you both and we'd love to have you over for a short visit tomorrow after open-gym. Ask your parents and, if that works out, we'll talk about a sleepover on Wednesday." The two boys hug Tina, hug me and race out of the gym.

As I get the props set up for our show, Tina figures out the *Lucy* theme on concertina. We'll do our dance number to a new tune tonight.

TUESDAY MORNING WE TALK with Pauline Agathluk, a teacher's aide and Yup'ik specialist, about adding some traditional stories into the show. She likes the idea but only works in the kindergarten and first-grade classrooms. It looks like the Emmonak show will have to be more circus and less stories than in Eek. I know I should care but I'm too road-weary — if these kids like circus, that's enough for me. Dougie and Barnsie are stars and the rest of the kids here are no slouches either. By Friday, their skills should be better than any other village we've visited.

After morning classes, walking to the lunch line, Dougie and Barnsie race up to hand us each an empty tray. Then they stand in front of us, smiling. Tina says, "I'm going to guess you're visiting us after school, am I right?" Eyebrows fly and wiggle. "Good." We start toward the line but the boys shift to stay in front of us. "Oh, there's more." Eyebrows up. "Now you want us to ask your parents if it's OK to sleep over tomorrow night?" Eyebrows up again. Tina says, "Alright, I'll visit your families tomorrow." Four eyes look at the floor. I try a different tack, "Maybe I should visit your families." Eyes up, eyebrows up. It seems the boys have this whole thing choreographed. I ask, "Whose family should I visit first?" Barnsie says, "You only need to go to Dougie's house; my mom said it was OK with her if it is OK with Dougie's family. Can you go today? Dougie has it all set up."

After school, while Tina is leading the open gym, I try to keep up with Dougie as he leads me to a two-story house near the river. We walk into the dark living room, where he introduces me to his father. Dougie disappears up the stairs and his father invites me into the kitchen, where an old man is sitting at the table sipping on an unlabeled beer bottle. "This is Dougie's grandfather." I put out my hand but the old man stares straight ahead, muttering in Yup'ik. He's a small, wiry man with straight salt-and-pepper hair. His plaid LL Bean shirt had once been green.

I sit at the table next to Grandpa while Father leans against the wall on the opposite side of the kitchen. I glance over my shoulder to see Dougie and two women, probably his mom and grandma, watching from halfway up the stairs. Grandpa suddenly grabs my arm. He's got strong fingers. He puts his face inches from mine and says, "I'm going to kill you." He's only got a few teeth and his breath reeks of Friday beer. I freeze, my mind racing through escape routes.

A moment later, Grandpa lets go of my arm, takes a sip and says, "Dougie's a good boy. He likes circus. You're OK." I exhale and look at the dad, who looks at the floor. Clearly, this is Grandpa's interview. I say, "Dougie is very good at circus."

"He's my grandson. He's a good boy." Another sip.

I peek over my shoulder and Dougie smiles at me. I notice a hunting rifle hanging on the wall over his head. Grandpa grabs my arm again. "I'm going to kill you." Another face-off; he lets go again and mutters about his grandson. I try to bring up the subject of a sleepover. Grandpa doesn't seem to hear me.

This pattern goes on for the next 45 minutes. I find myself getting bored with having my life threatened. I make a mental note that Yup'ik culture seems to be very patriarchal and deeply respectful of elders, even drunk ones. I tell myself that this is another real Eskimo experience and I wanted more of these — no tourist trinkets for me; just the real deal.

It is becoming clear that if I ever want to leave, I'm going to have to make a move. Grandpa lets go of my arm for the nth time and I quickly stand up. "Thank you, sir. It was a pleasure visiting with you. Now I have to go teach circus." I get out of the kitchen before he can grab me again and walk to the front door. Grandpa comes stumbling out, with Father right behind him. I say a quick good-bye to the rest of the family, open the door and my right bicep is in a vise. Grandpa turns me around and says, "I'm going to kill you" one more time. He's holding the rifle. Father looks horrified but doesn't move.

I go on automatic pilot. I say, "Good-bye, sir" and step into the arctic twilight. No gunshot.

I walk down three stairs and trudge through the deep snow. My back is tingling. I don't look.

No gunshot.

I try to convince myself that the old man is too drunk to hit me at this distance. I'm almost to the snowmobile path.

No gunshot.

I don't stop, I don't look back, I don't breathe until I'm inside the school. Standing in the hall, I hear Tina's voice coming from the gym. I made it.

I collapse on the floor, shaking and coated in sweat. I could have gotten shot in the back. That was a real gun and a really drunk man and he wanted to kill me. How did I manage to walk away? How did I survive? Two villages, two weeks, two chances to die of gunshot wounds. This is a whole lot more real than I really want.

Why did Dougie's grandpa want to kill me? Or was he testing me, some kind of *gussak* hazing ritual or a rite of passage? Or does he hate me for being a *gussak*, a clown who only thinks he's different from the racist teachers? Is he afraid I'll hurt his grandson? Was he even thinking about Dougie?

Why didn't someone stop him? What was the dad thinking? The way Dougie's mom and grandma cowered on the stairs makes me wonder what happens in that house when I'm not there. I imagine Grandpa drunk every night, smacking his family around. Maybe the whole family gets drunk, too.

I stop myself. What the hell am I doing? I've got a whole story going about Dougie's family, about "them." Get me a little scared and I start to think like the "dogs in heat" teachers. We've only been here two days and I'm turning into a Nazi.

I think back to Eek, to Paul Paul. He was my guide. Where is he now when I need him? He'd help me sort this out. Paul Paul is wise. And funny. A trickster, like Coyote or Raven.

Amazing; every road I go down leads to another cliché — the Drunk Eskimo, the Trickster, even the teachers are Those Bad White People. Have I seen anyone on this trip as a human being and not some version of "them" that I've got in my head?

The school door bursts open and Dougie comes charging in. He takes a couple of steps down the hall, stops, turns, and slides in to sit next to me.

"My grandpa really likes you. He said Barnsie and me can sleep over tomorrow! He might even come to see the show Friday and he never goes anywhere on Fridays 'cause it's beer day."

CHAPTER EIGHTEEN

VISITING
Emmonak

BARNSIE AND I GO IN for the last few minutes of open gym. After all
the other kids leave, Dougie and Barnsie clean up the equipment while
I give Tina the Cliff's Notes version of my visit with Grandpa. "He liked
you? Where I come from, firearms and death threats almost never say
'like.' Should we tell the boys we've changed our minds about the visit?"
I tell her I'm fine, that we would break their hearts.

At the apartment, Tina serves Dougie and Barnsie some sodas she
bought at the village store for the occasion and I make spam sliders. The
boys munch, drink and sit quietly. Tina and I sit with them. We don't
talk about grandpas or guns. We don't talk, period.

We are visiting.

Here in Eskimo country, words are not needed; being in a room
together is enough. At first I'm antsy and I see Tina fidgeting, but soon
we both settle in. It reminds me of the Quaker meetings my brother and
I got dragged to by our mother. Sitting in a room full of silent people for
an hour on a Sunday morning was torture for me, heaven for my mom.
Now I'm starting to feel what she must have felt — the joy of sharing
space with other human beings without expectations or tensions, letting
the world outside take care of itself for a few quiet moments.

The boys stand up, thank us and head home. I look at a clock — it's
been over two hours. Tina and I clean up and plan for tomorrow's classes
before falling into bed. No Lucy and Desi dance tonight.

THE WEDNESDAY NIGHT SLEEPOVER starts the same way as the

visit — some food, some soda and a lot of sitting. The boys tell us that their bedtime is 9 pm and that they want to hear circus stories before going to sleep. Tina tells them about a Bay City Reds show in a women's prison, before my time.

"As we were leaving, the prisoners asked us to sign some tennis balls. We weren't used to giving autographs and it swelled our heads a bit. I must have copped an attitude because one of the women said, 'Don't get all biggity; I just want something to sell if you ever get famous.'" The boys applaud at the end of the story and then make Tina explain the Reds' act to them throw by throw.

We get Dougie tucked in on the couch and Barnsie on a tumbling mat we borrowed for the night. Tina and I have decided to sleep in separate rooms — better to avoid gossip. Not ready to go to sleep and nervous in our new roles *in loco parentis*, we sit at the kitchen table. The boys are whispering together and we eavesdrop. They start talking about the tricks they're going to learn before the show on Friday. Then they drift into plans to go to Bethel or maybe even Fairbanks after they graduate. This sounds like a well-worn conversation, full of hope and ambition but devoid of specifics.

I realize how few dreams could come true for these boys. It doesn't matter how smart they are, how good they could be in a circus ring or how much they help each other. Bethel? To do what? Enlist in the military? Fairbanks? Maybe attend the university? Become teachers? Become drunks? Become so homesick they drop out and catch a mail plane to Emmonak?

They could try to follow Chuna McGinty, the one who got away, or Paul Paul, the one who came home. I imagine seeing them in San Francisco, street performing and auditioning for one of the local circuses. How would they get there? And what's in it for them? The real America? What if they stayed on out here on the Delta and got a gig touring villages teaching circus? They'd have to convince the Alaska Arts Council to get rid of the *gussaks* who currently have the job, of course. Are any of these dreams their dreams, or are they my dreams for them?

I realize I've missed the end of the boys' conversation, lost in my own thoughts. Tina kisses me on the cheek, puts a finger to her mouth and quietly goes to bed. I stand in the doorway looking at the sleeping boys. It's a sweet picture.

IN THE MORNING, AS THE FOUR of us are walking to school, Barnsie asks, "When are you leaving Emmonak?" Tina says, "We're going into Bethel Saturday morning and then to Anchorage on Sunday so we can catch an early flight Monday to San Francisco." The boys stop walking and look at each other. Dougie looks like he might cry. Barnsie says, "Could you go to Bethel on Sunday instead? There's something important happening at the community center on Saturday." The community center is a round, low-roofed wooden building in the middle of town that many people have pointed out but no one has invited us inside.

I ask, "Is it a potlatch?" We've heard about potlatches, days-long celebrations, often in late winter, when a few villages get together to dance traditional dances and eat the last of their winter stash. The boys look at each other again and Dougie says, "Kind of. It's a traditional celebration. You are invited. Special. You should come. Two o'clock on Saturday."

It's our turn to look at each other; I nod and Tina says, "Sure. I can call our boss and ask her to change the charter to Sunday morning. Thank you for inviting us." The boys beam, hug us both and race the rest of the way to school.

Tina says, "Looks like the trip home just got a little tougher." For me, thinking about the trip home has been tough for weeks: On one hand, I need to get back to get ready for theater school, if I get in, or to find another gig if I don't — this tour will pay next month's room and board but not much after that. At the same time, I'm more in love with Tina than I want to admit and I'm terrified that our tour romance won't last the plane rides south.

THURSDAY AFTER SCHOOL we are invited to an early dinner at a teacher's apartment next door to ours. A couple of other teachers arrive as we're eating pretzels and sipping smuggled Budweiser. The conversation turns, none too smoothly, to our sleepover last night and we pretty quickly realize this is more of an intervention than a party. Over deep-fried halibut and canned baked beans, Tina and I parry and thrust as the teachers accuse us of everything short of molesting the boys. We beg off before they serve dessert.

Back in our apartment, sipping tea in our little kitchen, Tina says, "Can't they keep their redneck noses out of our business?" I mention that the party is still going on the other side of a thin wall and she blows up: "I don't give a rat's ass — they're up here in Alaska making big money and hating on the kids they're supposed to be teaching. Then they have the nerve to lecture us." I agree, quietly, and try to calm her down. She goes to take a shower.

The teachers might be right to worry; we've heard rumors of kids getting molested. Even if they saw the sleepover for what it was, they would be right to be afraid that we're shaking things up, changing the relationship between teachers and students and then flying home when our week is up.

I hear the shower stop and then, a few minutes later, Tina goes into the bedroom she used last night and closes the door. It's quiet for a long time. I brush my teeth. I get in PJs. I listen at her door. I sit in the kitchen a while. I quietly open her door and peek in — it's dark except for the clock face, and Tina's breathing is deep and steady. I go to bed in the other room.

Tina's up early and has eggs and toast on the table, with black coffee, by the time I'm dressed. She gives me a kiss on the cheek, "Chow time. Eat up, we gotta make one last Tundra Circus, Emmonak-style." I want to ask her about last night but she's moving too fast, bubbly like I've never seen her before noon.

TEN HOURS LATER, the kindergarteners start the show by acting out a Yup'ik story told by Pauline Agathluk. The gym is packed, Eskimos and *gussaks*, and they are all in love with these little kids. Another story with the first-graders and then we're on to some hot circus acts: Barnsie leads a group of eight kids in a stilt dance, Dougie passes balls with two of his classmates and then does a solo club-juggling act, no drops, that ends with a 360 turn. The crowd goes wild. Two freshmen join Barnsie in a short unicycle act and, for our finale, the seniors make a couple of big human pyramids.

It seems like the whole village is hugging the kids after the show. I go over to meet Barnsie's family and get introduced to a bunch of other moms and dads, aunts and uncles, grandparents and cousins. Dougie's mom, dad and grandmother come over to congratulate me and I notice that Grandpa didn't show. I can't say I am disappointed, at least not for myself.

We hang around the gym until everyone's gone home except Pauline Agathluk, the Yup'ik language teacher. I think she wants to invite us over to visit but she doesn't say anything. After a while, we invite her to our place. She says, "yes," helps us finish packing and walks over to the apartment with us.

Pauline sits at our kitchen table drinking a cup of coffee; we sit with her, visiting. When she's halfway through her second cup, she quietly says, "It was good to have part of the show in Yup'ik." We sit quietly for another minute. "The other teachers tell me it's a waste of time. They say that Yup'ik is a dying language. Sometimes they say it isn't even a real language because it was never written down until Europeans came." Another pause. "It's hard."

We sit some more as I try to figure out something to say. Everything I'm thinking is either trite — "You're doing the best you can" and "Keep fighting the good fight" — or inappropriate. Tina finally says, "Your stories were my favorite part of the show. I think the kids would be excited if you did more of them in class next week."

"You think so? Maybe I'll try that." Pauline puts down her cup, thanks us and goes home. Tina takes my hand, "We did good."

"Yeah, we did."

"I'm beat. Let's go to bed."

I consider making a crack about "your room or mine" but decide that would make for a lonely night.

CHAPTER NINETEEN

BAR MITZVAH ON THE TUNDRA

Emmonak

SATURDAY MORNING WE SLEEP IN. It's almost eleven when I finally make breakfast — tundra lox and bagels (the last of our salmon strips with cream cheese on pilot bread). After we eat, Tina cleans the kitchen while I get the rest of the apartment ready for an early exit tomorrow. Then we walk over to the school to put the equipment into three piles — the stilts, juggling balls, rings, peacock feathers, costumes and makeup for the kids, all of which will stay at Stephanie's in Bethel; the props and costumes for our show, which are coming home with us; and then the unicycle and six juggling clubs, which we've decided to give to Dougie and Barnsie. Stephanie will probably throw a fit and try to make us pay for them, but it's worth it.

We're done at 2 pm, in time to walk over to the community center. The snow is muddy with footprints leading to the door. We step down into a large dark room dug into the ground. When our eyes adjust, we see a low amphitheater with a small fire in the middle. The place is full of people, at least a hundred of them, sitting quietly. Dougie runs over and leads us to an empty space a few rows up and right in the middle of the semicircle. He looks very proud in an ornate *kusbuk*. As soon as we sit down, an old man sitting on the far side starts speaking in Yup'ik. Dougie walks over and sits in front of him.

It takes me a few minutes to realize that the old man is Dougie's grandfather, dressed in a clean white shirt and tie. He sounds sober. He is leading a ceremony and Dougie is the focus of everyone's attention. I think, "This is a bar mitzvah" — or at least what would be a bar mitzvah if Dougie were Jewish. A young man's rite of passage. And they waited for us to begin, which means we're the honored guests. Tina and I share a moist-eyed look.

Grandpa keeps talking; Dougie sits quietly; all the guests sit quietly.

I never had a bar mitzvah; in fact we never went to temple. My mother would often tell the story of the day my father, who was raised Orthodox, asked our local rabbi how he should handle our questions about Christmas — we lived in an Italian Catholic neighborhood and Christmas was a big deal. The rabbi said, "Tell your boys that the fact they get eight presents on Chanukah makes Judaism eight times as good as Christianity." My father never set foot in a temple again.

Sitting in this community center in Emmonak, Alaska, watching a rite of passage for a 13-year-old boy who I've come to love in less than a week opens up something sweet in my secular heart.

The ceremony is changing and Dougie is coming over to us. Oh, shit, do we have to do something or say something in Yup'ik? I've seen people go up and butcher Hebrew in my cousins' bar mitzvahs and I swore never to do that. The only Yup'ik words I know are the names of some villages, a few greetings and my nickname, "Big Nose."

Dougie is smiling and handing me what looks like a dirty softball covered in Saran wrap. This is worse than having to speak. *Akutaq*. Eskimo ice cream, usually made of Crisco, sugar, frozen berries and fish. I give a big smile, take the package and do a Japanese-style bow over the *akutaq*. Dougie just stands there, looking from my face to the *akutaq*.

Oh, I'm supposed to eat some.

Right now?

Dougie raises his eyebrows.

I untwist the Saran wrap and the smell makes me gag. This isn't regular *akutaq*; it's traditional *akutaq* made with rancid seal oil instead of Crisco. Special treats for special guests. I smile again, a bit tighter, take two fingers and dip them into the mess.

The first taste is sweet, the sugar, and then the trouble begins — fish, cold berries, fish again and finally the six-month-old seal oil takes over, the arctic equivalent of past-its-expiration-date Limburger. Now I'm crying outright — and not for joy. Tina stifles a giggle. I could smash this whole thing in her face. Instead, I offer some *akutaq* to Dougie, which he reluctantly refuses; this treat is only for guests. I focus on breathing.

Dougie is now standing in front of Tina, handing her the biggest Hershey bar I've ever seen.

No fucking way.

Tina smiles, bows and opens up the bar. She offers a piece to Dougie, who again refuses but a little less reluctantly — clearly my *akutaq* is the main attraction. Tina eats a row of sweet squares.

I could kill her. Instead, I ceremoniously offer her some of my gift, what any good clown partner would do. Tina gives me a look that could melt permafrost and then looks at Dougie.

He is beaming — his new *gussak* friends are making such a good impression on his big day.

Tina takes a finger, dips out a dab of *akutaq* and then swallows it fast. The whole place applauds and it turns into a rhythmic clapping that gets faster and faster.

Oh god, they want an encore.

CHAPTER TWENTY

HOMEWARD BOUND
Anchorage Airport

TINA STAYS MAD ABOUT the *akutaq* — or maybe she was mad at me already and making her eat rancid seal oil only made it worse. Or maybe she's just sick of me or maybe she has a boyfriend hidden away in San Francisco and doesn't know how to tell me about him.

In any case, she doesn't speak to me after the ceremony and goes right into her bedroom when we get back to the apartment. She doesn't speak to me all day Sunday — the morning flight to Bethel with a tearful good-bye to Jenny, our final sauna (Stephanie sits between us) and a big lunch of caribou steaks and ptarmigan. She doesn't talk on our night flight to Anchorage or in the room with two beds at the airport hotel. She doesn't say, "We did it, we visited seven remote Eskimo villages, made some kids happy and didn't freeze to death or get shot." She doesn't say, "We'll never see Dougie and Barnsie again and that breaks my heart." She doesn't say, "Come over to my bed, boyfriend." She doesn't say anything.

When the alarm wakes us up at five o'clock on Monday morning, Tina pulls a pillow over her head. I go down to the lobby and bring up two cups of coffee, a peace offering, and then schlep all of our luggage down to the shuttle while Tina gets dressed.

We're at the gate at the Anchorage airport an hour before our flight to SFO. We don't need to be. The flight is delayed due to weather — fog in San Francisco.

Tina says, "Shit!"

I get her a double espresso and order a cappuccino for myself. It's overpriced airport coffee but this morning it tastes great. We sip and sit, looking out the window at our plane with the Alaska Airlines logo, an iconic Eskimo man, looking back at us from the tail. Tina downs the last thick drop, shudders and says, "I wonder if that old guy gets residuals every time a plane takes off." Happy to be talking, I say, "I wonder if he even realizes that they're using his picture on their planes." She says, "I wonder if anyone at Alaska Airlines knows his name or where to mail the residual checks if they ever wanted to pay him."

The P.A. system crackles to life:

> "Alaska Airlines flight 98 to San Francisco will begin boarding in 15 minutes. The weather at SFO is improving so we're going to get everyone on the plane and, hopefully, we'll get the all clear to head south to the City by the Bay. Estimated time of arrival is 11:15 am."

Tina and I hug each other, feel awkward and untangle without much grace. She says, "We're going home."

I say, "Yeah. I'll miss the kids."

"Me too."

"I'll miss you."

"Yeah. We did good together."

We sit for a minute. She says, "We're good as clown partners and the romance was sweet but it isn't going to work at home. We'll be apart too much, we'll get lonely and restless and one of us will take a sauna with someone else somewhere on tour and hearts will be broken. Been there, done that."

I stare at the handle of my carry-on. Part of me is crying and part of me is relieved. She's right, of course, and even if she wasn't, her mind is made up.

I say, "It's not fair, you know. You made me fall in love with you."

She snaps her head to look at me and then looks away.

I say, "But you're right; it won't work" and take a deep breath. "Tell you what, I'll make you a deal: You promise to keep working with me, to be my clown partner — no weirdness, no romance — and I promise not to make a huge scene right here in the airport, crying and screaming and kissing your feet and begging you to take me back. Deal?"

Tina grabs me in a bear hug and whispers "It's a deal, partner" and gives me a big kiss on the mouth.

"Whoa, not fair. Not fair at all."

Tina smiles, does a Groucho wiggle with her eyebrows and says, "All's fair in love and circus."

"Flight 98 for San Francisco is now boarding rows 20 to 30 through gate 52. Please have your boarding passes ready."

We check our boarding passes, row 14. I jump up and ask her to watch the stuff while I go find a pay phone to call my roommate; he's picking us up at the airport and I want to make sure he knows our new ETA.

I find a phone, put in two quarters and tell my roommate when we're supposed to arrive at SFO.

"Flight 98 for San Francisco is now boarding rows 10 to 20 through gate 52. Please have your boarding passes ready."

I say, "See you at SFO" and start to hang up when he says, "Oh, wait, you got something from Dell'Arte International. Want me to open it?"

My stomach knots up. "Sure."

"Let me go find it." The line gets quiet. The phone beeps. I dig into my pockets for another coin, find a dime and slide it into the slot.

"All rows for flight 98 are now boarding through gate 52. All rows please board now."

Finally, I hear rustling and my roommate says, "Got it. Sorry about that." The phone beeps. "Ok, I'll do this fast. Let's see, I'm reading the letter, 'Blah, blah, blah, accepted into Dell'Arte International School for the fall, blah, blah, blah, deposit due April 12, blah, blah, blah.' You're in, man!"

The line goes dead. I drop the phone and I race to catch my flight home.

ACT II
THE HEARTLAND
Lincoln, Nebraska
Spring 1995

CHAPTER TWENTY-ONE

A JEW IN THE HEARTLAND

IT IS YOM KIPPUR, the holiest day of the Jewish calendar, and I am doing a show in Lincoln, at the Johnny Carson Theater at the University of Nebraska. This is my first trip to the Heartland and my first tour as a playwright and actor. It's also a chance to bring my history, my family, my stories to a part of the country that seems even more remote than the Alaskan tundra.

My visit is starting with a full performance of my one-man show *Father-Land*. It's a comedy about the Holocaust and my father's suicide.

Light Cue 48: PHYSICAL CUE — Crossfade to Spotlight as the German Ringmaster stands on the chair

<u>German Ringmaster</u>
(accent like Joel Grey in Cabaret, *top hat)*

Ladies and gentlemen, boys and girls, *Meine Damen und Herren*, welcome to the center ring. You have seen the illusions, the sideshows, the affections, the passions, the pound of flesh nearest the heart.

Now I call your attention to this striking photograph. See the gravel yard in the foreground, the bunkhouses in the background, the shadow of the barbed wire on the wall. Look at that man, his tattered clothes hanging from his scarecrow frame. I need not insult your intelligence by saying "this man has suffered." The photograph burns his face into all of our minds...like a tattoo.

The barbed wire — who strung it? Who laid the bricks to build the wall? Did this Dachau brickmason really believe that his bricks were innocent bricks? Imagine his children, and his grandchildren and the shadow that barbed wire has cast on their lives.

Now, ladies and gentlemen, please, take one step back. Look at the whole photograph. Imagine taking that picture — "Just keeping a record." Imagine what it did to the picture taker. Imagine his children and his son's shock staring at that skinny man, and the shadow on the wall and suddenly seeing himself in that face. And then, suddenly seeing himself in his father.

Sound Cue 49: Music fade-in — Bach Cello Suite No. 1, Gigue

German Ringmaster tips the chair forward, landing on the stage standing. He juggles three silver balls to Bach Cello Suite.

Light Cue 50: PHYSICAL CUE — End of juggling act, bow and black out

The lights come back up, I slip the juggling balls into my pockets and take another bow. The 30 or so students who are still in their seats clap dutifully before grabbing their backpacks and jetting out. The theater is empty before I get offstage.

The work lights come on, I walk back out to thank the crew and start to pack up my props.

Father-Land is the first play I've written. The idea started in the Dachau museum, standing in front of photographs of emaciated prisoners. Walking through the sterile reconstruction of a bunkhouse with the other tourists hadn't stirred much emotion, which made me nervous — was I numb to genocide? Even the pictures didn't move me until I started to wonder if my dad had taken any of them; he was a photographer in the U.S. infantry, a 6' 4" 16-year-old who joined up, according to my aunt, "to save our race." The museum docent didn't have a list of photographers and my dad wasn't alive to tell me. A question formed in my head — what if my father took pictures of starving Jews and what if those pictures stayed in his head and eventually drove him crazy? — and it became the seed of a play.

Father-Land tells a story that is close to my heart. It is also my ticket, I hope, to more respect as an artist. I've worked in a lot of places since graduating from theater school over a decade ago — acting in a Moliere play in Montana, juggling in a skinhead bar in Germany, playing seven roles in Shakespeare's *Comedy of Errors* and going back up to Alaska a bunch of times — but I'm still always the "clown guy." *Father-Land* is personal and when it opened in San Francisco last year, the reviewers liked it (one even raved), but then nothing — no second run, no big producer picking it up for Broadway, like what happened to Whoopi Goldberg, nothing except this gig in Nebraska.

My job for the next seven weeks will be to help students "better understand and negotiate the diverse world of the university." A Mohawk poet was here before me; a Tejano trumpet player and a pioneer of African-American theater will be coming later in the school year. Good company, good work and a chance to be fully myself as an artist. On the other hand, Nebraska isn't Broadway.

I stash my chair, the hats and the juggling balls in a corner of the dressing room and go back onstage to strike the canvas backdrop. The theater is dark except for the "ghost light," a bare bulb on a five-foot stand placed in the center of the stage.

When I applied for this job a few months ago, I mentioned my trips to Yup'ik villages to show I had experience working cross-culturally. Then I put together a detailed syllabus, complete with lesson plans based on the "concept of 'stranger in a strange land' as the touchpoint between my Jewish experience and the students' experience coming to a large, diverse university from small homogeneous Nebraska towns." A good idea, I thought, and very academic sounding.

I got the job, and yesterday I met my boss Katharine, an elegant woman in her late 60s with sparkly blue eyes and smile lines all over her face that jump and play constantly. "Before you get going, I should mention that most of the students here have never met a Jew." I must have looked shocked because she laughed gently. "You're even going to find some folks who ask you to show them your horns and tail." Now it was my turn to laugh. But she said, "I'm not exaggerating, unfortunately. It'll be hard to take them seriously but you will need to. If you come on like some big-shot artist from San Francisco, they'll clam up so fast you'll think you're at a funeral." She picked up my syllabus and looked at me with her eyes twinkling. "We're lucky to have you. I'll help you tweak your lesson plans tomorrow. Let's go get some lunch at the Student Center and then head over to the theater to tech your show."

Since I'm now a professional Jew, I should have realized that the only full performance of *Father-Land* was booked on Yom Kippur, a day of fasting and rest. I should have refused to do the show; Sandy Koufax refused to pitch a World Series game on Yom Kippur.

I'm not Sandy Koufax.

I didn't cancel the show, arguing in my head, and to my fiancée, that I *had* to perform *Father-Land*. "It is more Jewish to do this show for these students than to cancel for arcane religious laws that I don't believe in." My fiancée was raised Jewish, bat mitzvah and all, and she's not a performer. She didn't buy "the show must go on" but, when she realized that I wasn't cancelling the performance, she figured out a way to celebrate Yom Kippur at the theater: A couple of scenes ago she slipped out into the lobby with my aunt, a UNL professor, and they are now serving the audience sliced apples and honey, Jewish symbols of a sweet new year. By the time I join them, still in costume and covered in sweat, the food is gone and the lobby is empty.

My aunt says, "The kids who walked out early said some nasty things — 'I won't eat your Jew food' and the like — but then one of them couldn't resist and pretty soon we had a line. A nice, neat line since this is Nebraska. Sugar is the great unifier."

CHAPTER TWENTY-TWO

GUILT OF THE FATHER

Light Cue 16: PHYSICAL CUE — when the glasses are on, crossfade to Ghost Father light

Ghost Father
(New York accent, round glasses)

Ghost Father uses the chair as a tripod, miming a camera; he makes a sound like a camera click

That was a great shot; the light was perfect. See the shadow of the barbed wire just off his chin then it hits the wall at that great angle. What a face.

I was setting up my tripod to shoot the shadow on the wall, simple, when this guy, doesn't speak a word of English, comes up and wants to play with my equipment. He's half dead and he wants to take my camera apart. So I try to get him to stand for a picture but he says something in Yiddish that doesn't sound exactly polite and starts to walk away. I yell at him, "Hey, buddy" and he looks back for a second. Click. I get the shot.

Luck. The right place at the right time.

The right place? It was a little tough, keeping my mind on the photography, not getting caught up with the subjects and the setting and everything. Documentation, that's all. A little tough, just kept my mind on the light, the F-stop, the depth of field. It was hard.

Ghost Father balances the chair on his foot

Of course, we only spent a few hours a day at Dachau shooting, taking pictures. Then we'd go back to the base. The war was over, the Germans were defeated. I had a pass, could go into town any time. There were even a few stores open — all these German mothers going shopping with their fat little kids. I started getting the feeling that we hadn't won the war. These kids were going to grow up hating Jews, hating *my* kids. It's not just gonna stop. What's to keep this whole mess from happening again?

I told my buddies the truth about the Germans: "Germans are animals. They are basically bad." My buddies didn't care. They just wanted to get home to their girlfriends. They knew they had won the war. They couldn't see what was right in front of their eyes: Germans were going to keep on killing Jews; it's part of their psyche.

Well, no one wanted to hear that. Didn't seem to bother anyone else, so I kept to myself, kept my mind on the photography. It was hard.

Ghost Father balances the chair on a hand

So, anyway, 1946 I shipped out stateside, left it all behind. Went back to school, met my wife, got a PhD. Settled into an academic life. Living in Rochester, New York. Doing fine.

One day, in the early '50s, I was coming home from the library, late afternoon, typical Rochester winter. In the park, on a bench, I see this skinny guy, too small for his coat, five o'clock shadow, hunched over.

I freeze. I'm figuring where the light is coming from, how I'll frame this one up. I'm taking pictures in my mind.

All of a sudden I hate this skinny guy, *hate* him. And then I remember — I hated those people. No, I'm not talking about the Nazis. I hated the Jews: they smelled bad, made me sick trying to touch me. Couldn't they tell I was a fraud? Hell, there I was, this big healthy Jewish boy, taking pictures, *taking pictures* of the extermination of his own race. "Just keeping a record." And they were thanking me like I was their savior. I hated them, "Leave me alone!"

After that, it got hard, every day, seeing people in the street, in class. Framing them up. Trying not to get mad. Keep my mind on my work. Keep my family together. It was hard.

Ghost Father balances the chair on his chin

Light Cue 17: Fade to black

I TAKE A LITTLE BOW and sit down on the chair, the same sleek metal style used on the set of every TV cop show. The students scattered around the theater clap loudly. This is my first class, all acting students, and they seem to like the scene from *Father-Land*. They're studying solo performance — John Leguizamo, Lily Tomlin, Sir Ian McKellen, even Whoopi Goldberg before she became a movie star.

My boss Katharine brings me a cup of water and goes to get herself a chair. I start talking to the students about techniques for writing solo material and how to create fiction from life. I tell them about taking a fact — my father was a photographer in the infantry during World War II — and creating a scene about a fictional photograph. I tell them about finding a real artifact — a letter my father sent to his mother on VE day — and using some of the language in a fictional scene ("…all these German mothers going shopping with their fat little kids."). I tell them about creating an entirely made-up event — my father having a flashback of the war when he sees a skinny man in Rochester — to give a hint about his real suicide years later.

The students are nodding and taking notes so I start to explain how I integrated circus skills as metaphor, like balancing the chair when my father was obviously unbalanced. I take a breath and Katharine says, "You've given us a lot to think about." She looks at the audience. "I wonder if anyone has any questions so far." A bunch of hands shoot up and Katharine calls on them one at a time.

"How old were you when your dad killed himself?"

"What do you remember about your father?"

"How did your mom deal with it?"

"How did he do it? Kill himself, I mean?"

I'm taken aback. I thought that theater students would want to talk about theater, about art, but all they want to know is how Daddy killed himself. I don't want to talk about my family; I want to talk about my play.

It was hard enough writing *Father-Land:* Reading my father's journals as he fell into depression, looking at the pictures he took during the war, hearing the family stories about why he killed himself — it was my mother's fault, it was just a chemical imbalance, he hadn't won a Nobel Prize yet. No one even considered that walking around Germany with a Winchester in his hand and a Kodak Retina 2 around his neck might have done some damage to his teenaged brain.

Katharine says, "So, why don't you tell us more about you father."

I want to say, "You don't get it! I'm telling a story about a Jewish American photographer at Dachau, an artist alone in a strange land trying to understand genocide and all you want is family gossip" — but I don't.

I keep my mind on the questions; keep my answers short and simple.

The class finally ends. A few students come up to chat before racing off to their next class.

Katharine shakes my hand and says, "Nice work." I mumble, "It was hard" and she nods, "Oh, yes, it's always hard. That's why we bring artists here; you like to play with the hard stuff — ambiguity, images, metaphors, pain."

"But they weren't interested in my images and metaphors." I hear an ugly whine creeping into my voice but I can't stop myself. "They weren't interested in the art at all — they just wanted to hear about my mom and dad. You don't need me for that; anyone can talk about their family."

Katharine says, "You're not giving them much credit" without an edge in her voice. "They listened to your lecture on fiction writing. They even took notes." Her laugh lines are dancing. "Then you got them talking, which is no mean feat here in Nebraska. That's a great start. Now let's get grab a quick lunch — we've got another class in 45 minutes."

I perform the same scene for the next class, more theater students, and let Katharine lead a Q&A right afterward, no lecture. They ask about my family and add a few questions about the business of show business. They're talking, Katharine's happy and I'm getting more comfortable. I will be on my own for the next two days since Katharine has to deal with an emergency — a Brazilian dance company is in town and it turns out that all of the dancers, men and women, perform bare-chested, putting the planned student matinee in jeopardy.

Starting with the Wednesday morning class, I get in a groove, even finding a few moments to talk about the play while ostensibly answering questions about my family. By Thursday evening, I feel like I might be earning my paycheck — the students are getting to know me, a Jewish artist, which might, by some rough magic, help them "negotiate the diverse world of the university."

Katherine Vernon sits at her desk, long legs stretched out, talking with her daughter in Florida. She cherishes these moments: the feel of the phone and the crackle of the long-distance line reminds her of when she was the new bride of a successful salesman. He called every day, no matter where he was in the world. Every day.

As her daughter, now married herself, talks about the new house and the crazy neighbors, Katherine is back 40 years catching a quick call with her lover across mountains and oceans.

"I love you, too, dear. Call me tomorrow."

Back to now, back to here, back to work.

The Brazilians left this morning, thank god. She loved them, loved their show and loved, loved, loved watching the kids at the matinee, the ones who've had a local dancer visit their school every week for months. Those little guys jumped into the aisle and danced right along with the pros; pure magic. Nebraskan children matching step for step with sleek, sexy Brazilians. The kids didn't smile — this was serious, this was their chance to dance. The rhythms are now theirs, part of their lives, part of their bodies, not the strange, scary moves their parents see.

The parents are why Katherine is glad the troupe is winging their way back to Sao Paulo. She hates the thought of these beautiful artists seeing the ugly side of Lincoln. She had managed the bare-breast dilemma without too much vitriol reaching the dancers, but if they'd have stayed even one more day she was sure it would have been bad. Sometimes she wishes she worked in another town, somewhere more worldly. Then she thinks of the kids and the Brazilians, dancing together, and knows she's in the right place, making magic on the border between worlds.

The phone rings, Katherine sighs and picks up the receiver. It takes a lot of phone calls to make a little magic.

CHAPTER TWENTY-THREE

HOME OF THE CHIEFS

A UNL SENIOR NAMED CHET, who's my go-to driver, steers his battered blue Ford pickup into the parking lot of the Omaha Nation Public School. I'm finishing my first week with a short field trip out of Lincoln, visiting this school near the town of Macy on the Omaha Reservation. We park, get out and stare at a big sign that reads "Home of the Chiefs" under a logo that looks shockingly like the NFL's infamous Redskin.

Chet says, "A few years ago, this place was rated the worst high school in America." He talks and dresses like central casting's idea of a fifth-generation Nebraska farmer, which is what he is.

"That's a good thing to mention right now. Thanks, Chet."

"Don't worry, man, they've got a new principal and one of the history teachers just graduated from UNL. She's cool. You'll have a ball."

Karen Anderson is in her first month of teaching and, from the size and color of the bags under her eyes, it had been a hard month. Her classroom is postered with presidents, maps and other images from European American history. A couple of students are hanging around before class, so Karen introduces me to one of them, a rotund junior named Vernon Wolfe. Vernon's face is pear-shaped with a couple of jowly chins and ears as big as the Buddha's. My first thought is that he looks like an ox; his expression is distinctly bovine. He asks me, "Why are you here?" sounding completely bored.

"I'm with a program out of the University of Nebraska and I'm teaching here today."

"Oh. What do you teach?" His monotone flattens out an accent that would be at home in an Eskimo village.

"I'm going to teach storytelling today; I'll tell some stories and then I'll invite you to tell your stories."

"Oh. Do we get paid for our stories?"

Looking at his lifeless face, I am beginning to wonder if Vernon is developmentally delayed. I laugh and say, "No, we'll just share stories and learn about each other. I would like to learn about your life here on the Omaha Reservation."

Vernon's face instantly comes to life — sharp eyes, a little smile on his lips — and he says, without a trace of an accent, "I bet you get paid for your stories, don't you?"

I blush and stutter out something ridiculous about working for the university, which means I have to get paid. Before I'm done, Vernon's face is back to its "dumb Indian" mask.

"Oh. I understand. Thanks."

THE MORNING IS A SERIES of tired teachers trying to control rowdy classes. The kids are wary of me and the classrooms devolve into chaos every time I ask them to do an activity — telling stories, acting them out, even doing a little scarf juggling. One girl, a cool-kid senior named Tillie, challenges everything I say and offers heated, and clever, arguments for why she shouldn't join in. She reminds me of a much quieter but equally stubborn Eskimo girl who beat me in basketball years ago. By lunch, even Chet's chipper chatter can't get me excited about going to the fifth-period class.

Amazingly, Tillie is the bright spot of the afternoon. She comes into a sophomore English class just as I am trying to get the students to act out a story. She joins right in and the other kids follow her lead. Soon Tillie is teaching all the exercises she had argued against in the morning. She is good and the kids are into it; I mainly watch. When the bell rings, I thank Tillie and ask if she wants to come to my next class. "Can't. Gotta go to math or they'll flunk me. Besides, you just saw me do it — you should have been taking notes." Tillie winks and runs out the door.

After school, I'm scheduled to lead a workshop for the teachers. Chet gets me to the site a little early, a bungalow a couple of muddy blocks from the school. About 30 chairs are set in a circle and a coffee machine gurgles on a table near the door. At the start time, there are only a handful of teachers, all women, and a man in his fifties who introduces himself as Clifford Porter. He says he's a member of the Tribal Council.

"We're going to start late; most of the teachers are at a funeral. Might last a while. Funerals are important in Indian Country."

"Of course. I completely understand."

"How did your day go at the high school?"

I give Clifford a thumbnail version, highlighting Tillie and skipping Vernon. "I just wish that all the classes had participated the way that one class did with Tillie. Most of them didn't seem to trust me."

"So, tell me, are you going to be here tomorrow?"

"No, we have to get back to Lincoln tonight, I've got classes…"

"I know." Clifford's voice is now sharp and hard. "Do you think these kids are stupid? Do you have any idea how many people come here for one day and then leave? Do you know how many people have betrayed these kids? They'd have to be pretty stupid to trust a white man in one day." His face softens just a little, "Tillie must have seen something in you. If you were here for a month, maybe even less than that, the kids might start to do your exercises on their own. But our kids are not stupid."

All the time I've spent teaching in Eskimo villages should have prepared me for the Omaha Nation School. I should have known they wouldn't, couldn't trust me any more than the Eskimo kids could reveal their secret names. I'm in Nebraska telling stories about my family and the Holocaust; these kids' lives are shaped by a different holocaust and I'm on the wrong side of that story.

CHAPTER TWENTY-FOUR

OUR HOUSE

Light Cue 21: PHYSICAL CUE — when the wig is on, dip fade to Helga light

<u>Helga (young German woman)</u>
(light German accent, red Mohawk wig)

Good morning, *Mein Jüdische* Actor from America. No, no, don't get out of bed; I'll make the tea.

I've been reading your play, *The Merchant of Venice*. Shylock and Portia and the pound of flesh.

I know that Shakespeare story. Let me tell you another story, a *true* story.

When I was a little girl, one day I come home from school and in front of my house is a man, standing there. I was a brave little girl, I go up to him — he was old, with a big coat and a beard and a nice hat. I ask him "Why are you looking at my house?" He jumps when I talk to him, like he is caught being bad. He says, "I used to live in that house."

I like this man because he is sad and I like sad people. I take his hand and lead him into my house. He walks around staring at everything. In my room he stands and stares at my bed for a long time and then he says,

"No, her bed was over there." Before I can ask him who he is talking about, my mother comes in and she says "Who are you?" to the old man. He says, "You are living in my house!"

My mother smiles a little. "I'm sorry, you are mistaken, this house has been in my family for many years. You are perhaps confused with the other houses on the block." But the old man says, "No, no, I am not mistaken." He looks at me, "You have a beautiful daughter. Good day."

After the old man left, my mother scolded me for letting him in. She said I must be careful who I talk with, he could be dangerous. This was funny to me because he was so old and sad looking, but now I know why she was scared — he was a Jew.

This old man, this old Jew, his name was Stern. I found this out when I was 14 years old. I could never forget him and his "You are living in my house!" I had to know who he thought of when he stared at my bed. I know, a crazy idea.

Light Cue 22: Slow crossfade (15 count) to cold wash

I look at all the papers in the city records, beginning when I was 11 years old. I was very smart, a little lawyer. Like Portia. Everyone thought I was a crazy little girl, but one day I found a paper.

That night, after I do the dishes, I make my parents sit back down at the kitchen table; I put the paper in front of them and say: "In our house lived Rachel Stern, age 34, David Stern, age 37, and their beautiful daughter Anna Stern, age 7. Arrested: 3 September, 1941. Deported: 5 September, 1941. Official death of the mother and daughter: 12 December, 1943. Father officially missing."

I said, "Mother, your dear, charming father, my

grandfather, and our perfect Aryan family moved into this house 6 September, 1941, the day after the Sterns were deported. *The day after!*"

I asked my parents, "Do you want me to go on? Can you really tell me that you knew nothing about this?"

They just stared at me. They didn't say anything.

Finally, my mother said, "You are perhaps confused with the other houses on the block," and I started screaming.

The next few years were hard; my parents refused to take my side against my grandfather, the monster with an explanation for everything. I didn't think that our house was ours; we stole it from Mr. Stern and we owed him a debt, like the pound of flesh in *Merchant of Venice*. My parents didn't want to believe it.

Light Cue 23: Slow fade to black

I SIT ON THE LIP OF THE STAGE; no bow necessary since no one is clapping. It's Monday morning so the students may still be hung over from the Cornhusker's home game on Saturday. I'm starting my second week, moving on to classes outside of the theater department. I chose the Helga monologue from *Father-Land* because these students are studying 20th-century history. I thought it would resonate.

I'm not seeing a lot of resonating.

Katherine, after solving the crisis of the bare-chested Brazilians (bikini tops), is hard at work scheduling the next artists. My fiancée has gone home to San Francisco and my aunt has a full teaching load so there are no apples and honey to distract the students. I'm on my own.

After a few moments the professor, a tall, dark-haired woman about my age in a tailored grey jacket and matching slacks, sits next to me and asks the students if they have any questions about the scene I just performed. They look at us without a flicker of interest. I try to imagine what they were thinking watching a big Jewish actor in a red wig pretending to be a German girl obsessed with real estate. No wonder they are just staring.

The teacher reminds them about the readings they've done on World War II. Light bulbs don't go off. Finally, she gets one young man with short-cropped blond hair and a long face to speak. "Why did you make this Helga lady so hung-up on her house? Who cares who lived in it before they did?"

The prof exhales and starts a short lecture on German citizens cooperating in, and benefiting from, the deportation of Jews. A few students take notes — this might be on the test. The professor turns and asks me about my research for the role. Relieved that she's taking the lead, I tell her about reading *Born Guilty*, a book of interviews with the children and grandchildren of Nazis. I'm starting to explain how I created Helga from a few of these stories when the students all stand up and leave. They are responding to the silent alarm that goes off in college kids' heads when class is over.

In less than a minute, the professor and I are alone in the theater. I stare at the empty seats. The professor stands up, thanks me and adds, "These kids are from really small towns. They know a whole lot about their families and farming and the Huskers but not a lot about history. And nothing about Jews."

I go back to my apartment a few blocks from campus and eat leftover pad thai for lunch. I'm homesick and defeated. My aunt helped me get this gig and she was so excited that I was bringing some Jewishness to Lincoln. I'm glad she didn't see me this morning.

CHAPTER TWENTY-FIVE

FAMILY SECRETS

Light Cue 25: Spotlight on Helga's Grandfather

Helga's Grandfather
(thick German accent, green Bavarian hat)

Curious girl, my granddaughter Helga. She has always been very smart, ever since she was small. Our house was of particular interest to her. One day she found a document, it was no doubt accurate, which said that people called the Sterns had lived in our house. They moved out and we moved in. I did not know these people, but my granddaughter seemed to think I had something to do with their deciding to move, that maybe I threw them out of their house.

I could not throw anyone out of their house. I was a poor man. My family and I lived in a small apartment. One day a friend of mine, who sold real estate, told me about a big house for a good deal and I bought it. I didn't throw anyone out. Is it a crime to want a nice house for your family? Would you have done anything different? I don't think so.

Helga says this Mr. Stern visited our house years later, when she was a little girl, so he must have survived the war just fine. Perhaps he went to America, along

with some of the other Jews, and came back for repara-
tion money. I don't know.

Reparations. I think about reparations often. Helga's Mr. Stern fascinates me. He must be about my age,
healthy and wealthy enough to travel a long way just
to see an old house. I would have liked to meet him
when he came, but I was in hospital. Did Helga mention that I spent a lot of time in hospital? It wasn't what
you would think — the years in prison — that ruined
my health. No, no, the three years from the end of the
war, 1945, until I was arrested in 1948; they were the
worst: the accusations, the lawyers, the neighbors suddenly telling evil stories about me. Constantly being
followed, questioned by the police. Prison was almost a
relief after that torture.

When I got out of prison, Germany was in the middle of the "economic miracle," but no one wanted to
hire a sick, middle-aged jailbird. It was very hard until the children were grown. Of course, we got no help
from the government. No reparations for us. You see,
sometimes I wonder about reparations.

My children are grown and doing well; they are the new
Germany. I am forgotten, and this is how is should be —
what do we gain from living in the past? Germany is the
richest and hardest-working country in the world. We
are one country again, one *Deutschland*. After achieving
so much, why must we constantly be reminded?

Of course, if my granddaughter had her way, I would
suffer for some imagined crimes. Helga brings you
here, a Jew, thinking that when I see you I remember
my crimes. What crimes? No, when I see you I do not
feel guilty. I feel angry. I know, it is childish, but I see a
big healthy Jewish boy from the Golden Land of America, standing there, judging me. Let me tell you, I owe
you nothing. I am guilty of nothing!

Light Cue 26: Dip fade to warm wash

I DECIDED TO TRY A DIFFERENT SCENE this afternoon but I'm still getting blank stares. I should have done the Helga monologue first to at least give some context for her grandfather's scene. Maybe wearing a little Bavarian hat and spewing subtle lies in a fake German accent isn't the best way to reach these students.

Now that I'm out of the theater department, I've got nothing in common with these kids. I'm dying to do *Father-Land* in a real theater again, for an audience that wants to be there, instead of cutting my play into little pieces and trying to feed them to students who don't care.

In the absence of any questions, I find myself railing against the folks, like the Grandfather character, who passively supported Hitler. The students' eyes glaze over. This is a law class, of all things, so I pivot to the question of establishing guilt — is the Grandfather guilty, legally or morally, for moving into the Sterns' house?

The professor perks up. He's an elegant man with a gray mane wearing a dark-green tweed suit and a purple bow tie. We have a short debate about the Grandfather's guilt. The prof's judgment: it looks suspicious but not enough evidence to convict in an American court.

Now that I have the professor talking, I bring up *Merchant of Venice* to try to keep him going. "After all of Portia's poetry about the quality of mercy, she tries a cheap legal trick to foil the Jew Shylock." I hop up on stage and give a few of Portia's lines from Act IV, when she's disguised as a lawyer out to convict Shylock:

> This bond doth give thee here no jot of blood;
> The words expressly are 'a pound of flesh:'
> Take then thy bond, take thou thy pound of flesh;
> But, in the cutting it, if thou dost shed
> One drop of Christian blood, thy lands and goods
> Are, by the laws of Venice, confiscate
> Unto the state of Venice."

I ask, "Would that argument stand up in any court you know?"

The prof laughs and says, "No, it wouldn't. It only works in fiction. But remember that the Bard never met a Jew or at least never met an 'out' Jew since they were outlawed in England at the time. And the play is set in Venice, where Jews were considered aliens by law." He turns to the class. "The word 'ghetto' comes from the Jewish quarter in Venice." A few of them take notes. "Now, if I remember correctly, after Portia's legally suspect trick about blood and flesh, she goes in for the kill." He strides center stage, strikes a ballet fourth position, raises his right hand and, in a booming voice that speaks to years on the debate team, intones, "*The Merchant of Venice*, act five, scene one."

> "Tarry, Jew:
> If it be proved against an alien
> That he seek the life of any citizen,
> The party 'gainst the which he doth contrive
> Shall seize one half his goods; the other half
> Comes to the privy coffer of the state;
> And the offender's life lies in the mercy
> Of the duke only."

This guy knows his Shakespeare and he's not half bad as an actor. We trade *Merchant* monologues and the students get interested, if only for the novelty of watching their teacher emote instead of litigate. The tweedy prof and I keep going even after the silent alarm goes off and the theater empties.

AFTER GRABBING A BURGER at the student union, I decide to treat myself to a movie. The Lincoln Grand Cinema is playing *Life Is Beautiful* with Roberto Benigni. I get a ticket and sink into a plush red seat in the back row, holding an extra-large buttered popcorn in my lap.

Soon Benigni is riding a bicycle across the countryside as a 1940s version of the classic Italian clown Arlecchino and it makes me deliriously happy. He is so light and sharp, a Chaplin for the 21st century. 10 minutes in and I'm in love with his character and the movie.

Now the scene turns urban and darker.

Now it's the early days of World War II.

Now men are being taken away by soldiers.

If Benigni goes to a concentration camp, I'm walking out of the theater.

Benigni is now in a camp and my heart's breaking and I can't stop watching. He's still funny, thank god, and tragic and light and heavy and my skin is crawling and I'm crying and finally the lights come up.

I sit there, staring at the rolling credits. The couple in front of me are talking. He says, "What was that place he was living in, with all the skinny men? I didn't get that part." His girlfriend starts to explain what the Holocaust was. I stand up, stumble out of the theater into the crisp spring night and start to walk home.

I want to be Roberto Benigni. I want to make a movie like his. I want my movie to tour in Nebraska, not me.

CHAPTER TWENTY-SIX

TAQUERIA MEXICANA

"DAMN…THIS…CHICKEN…is…good." I'm sitting on a plastic chair in Taqueria Mexicana in Grand Island, Nebraska. My mouth is stuffed with shredded chicken floating in spicy, rich, chocolaty *mole poblano*, a sauce that, when cooked slowly and with skill, makes my mouth happier than almost anything else on Earth.

"See, I told you so." Chet's smile lights up his farm-boy face. He's barely touched his *chile rellenos,* choosing instead to watch me eat and whisper "I told you so." He's right; he did tell me so.

On Tuesday morning, Chet picked me up, after I'd barely survived a long night of replaying *Life Is Beautiful* in my head, to start this four-day tour of rural schools. As I got into his old Ford pickup, Chet handed me a paperback guide to restaurants across Nebraska. "We're only gonna eat Mexican and only at restaurants in old gas stations. I've got them marked on the map and starred in the book. You navigate."

I had to tell him that I've lived in the Mission District of San Francisco for almost 20 years and my iron-clad rule is to never eat Mexican food outside of California. Chet was completely unfazed. Somehow he convinced me to try a three-table affair in an old Phillips 66 station in Beaver Crossing, less than an hour west of Lincoln. I didn't dare order *mole* in that first joint but the *tamales* were so good I purred. Since then, he's been trying to get me to eat *mole* everywhere we go. "You will love it. Mark my words."

Now he's gloating. "I told you that they do good *mole* out here. I've *been* telling you but do you listen? Noooo." Chet's laugh echoes through the nearly empty restaurant. "How come you're so picky about *mole* anyway?"

Between bites of chicken and sips of *horchata*, I tell Chet about a time in the mid-eighties when I was touring California with a small circus. We had stopped to get lunch at El Ranchito in Riverbank, a farming town in the Central Valley. El Ranchito was two mobile homes welded together and plopped down on a patch of dirt. The *mole poblano* was so heavenly that Tina and I made the waiter bring out the chef. After some hemming and hawing, the young man walked out of the kitchen with an ancient woman in a white apron and hairnet. "My *abuela* doesn't like to leave the stove." We stuttered, "*Muchas gracias por el mole*," hopped up on a table and passed seven clubs, each club nearly grazing the ceiling. I did a pile-up, catching the last club between my legs, and the restaurant went crazy. Still holding the club between my legs, I hopped around in time to see the chef walking slowly back into the kitchen. Not a word. We decided she was our Yoda and from that moment on, El Ranchito's *mole poblano* has been my gold standard.

"Does this match El Ranchito?"

"Not quite, but the old Esso sign kicks the décor onto another level. Now eat your *rellenos*."

The reason the Mexican food in rural Nebraska is good is the same reason El Ranchito is good: jobs that most Americans won't do. In California, it's a more complex history (not so long ago, of course, California was part of Mexico), but the basic concept still holds: Most of El Ranchito's customers are farmworkers who pick broccoli and tomatoes, grapes and garlic in the scorching Central Valley sun for minimum wage at best; most of Taqueria Mexicano's customers arrived in Grand Island in the last decade, coming here for jobs in the meatpacking plants that dying Nebraska towns thought would kick-start their economies. The town fathers soon found that meatpacking jobs are too dangerous, low-paying and smelly for most folks in small-town Nebraska, paving the way for Chet and me to eat great Mexican food sitting next to rusting gas pumps in Kearney, Scottsbluff, Nebraska City and now Grand Island.

When we weren't eating, my job was to visit classrooms, mainly high school, to perform and start discussions about diversity. We're the thin edge of the wedge for UNL rural outreach and recruiting. The first class in the first town, Kearney, was freshman history and they greeted me with a round of applause. A good start. The teacher, a young man in jeans and a button-down white shirt, almost leapt across the room to shake my hand. "We've been doing all the pre-reading about Jews and we've figured out there are two and a half Jews in our school." He was so excited and I was so confused that all I could say was, "Great." "We know that Bobby Levin and Danny Newman are Jewish and we think that Jenny Meyer might be Jewish. So that's two and a half Jews." The students were great — curious, engaged, friendly — so I didn't nitpick about their math.

In other towns, the ones with meatpacking plants, once home to descendants of European immigrants exclusively, now full of new immigrants with darker skin, a different sound and spicier tastes, "diversity" is an open wound. The white kids, who were game to talk about the Holocaust, anti-Semitism, even suicide, got vicious when the conversation turned to "the Mexicans." The Mexican-American kids were just as angry and hurt. My first attempt to give a historical perspective, mentioning that 70 years ago the local Ku Klux Klan became popular on an anti-immigrant, anti-Catholic and anti-German platform, was met with a particularly Nebraskan kind of silence — neutral, patient and stubborn.

To break the silence, I turned to stories, their stories. In one town, a white girl told about going into a video store only to find all the titles were in Spanish. When she went to the counter to ask for movies in English, the family running the store, including a classmate, walked into the back room laughing and talking in Spanish. "This is America. Why can't I get American movies here? Why should I have to listen to these people making fun of me in a language we don't speak in Nebraska?"

I resisted saying anything and just asked for another story, pointedly looking at the other side of the room. A Mexican-American girl, who may have been the classmate in the first girl's story, told about being called "wetback," "greaser" and "fucking Mexican whore" as she sat at the counter every day after school, ringing up video rentals and trying to do her homework. "My *papá* used to take a break when I got there but now he's too scared to leave. After some drunk white guys tried to grab me a few weeks ago, he started keeping his gun under the counter."

The stories didn't thaw the room and I'm sure my half-day visits didn't make life better for these kids. Chet says we're doing our job just by showing up and getting them talking about really hard subjects. I'd love to believe him.

"Hey, it's Friday, we worked hard, let's get dessert! We need to celebrate your big tour of small-town Nebraska. On UNL's tab, of course." Chet calls the waiter over and says, "We'll take some custard, two spoons."

Our dessert arrives, a hefty quarter round with a dark-brown top and golden sides. When the waiter sees my curious look, he says, "It's *flan de cajeta*. Special. With caramel."

The long drives and the tough classes melt away as the rich, sweet flan slides down our throats.

CHAPTER TWENTY-SEVEN

GHOST FATHER

Light Cue 28: PHYSICAL CUE — when the glasses are on, crossfade to Ghost Father light

<u>Ghost Father</u>
(in round glasses, speaking to his son)

I grew up in Rochester, New York, a nice Jewish family. I joined the army in 1944, didn't see too much action in the war; I was a photographer. When I got home, I went to college, met my wife and became a physicist. Unfortunately, I had a chemical imbalance that made it impossible for me to work after a few years, so I considered what it would be like to live in institutions and I decided to take my own life.

That's my prepared speech. That speech kills me, pardon the expression. I didn't even mention you kids in it. I loved you kids, loved you. How could I leave you out of the story of my life? My résumé. Insensitive, that's what it is.

Ghost Father sits in the chair

Typical, perfectly typical. Never change. Depressing.

He almost falls out of the chair

Whoa, let's not go down that road.

He stands up

> You remember the motorcycle? That was a great bike, a custom, extra-long seat for you boys. Even got you little helmets with little straps on them. We were going to drive that bike to California, remember? Flying across the Heartland, me and my boys. 'Course your mother wouldn't let us go, said you were too young. Hell, you were what, six, seven? That's too young?
> ...five...three? Really? That's young. You were practically babies, what the hell was I thinking? How were you going to hold on, the two of you with your little arms. Stupid, really stupid.

Ghost Father sits in the chair

> Typical, perfectly typical. Never change, insensitive. Depressing.

He almost falls out of the chair

Whoa, let's not go down that road.

He stands up

> The war, you asked about the war, right? The war was fine, really. Great. Does that sound strange? Let me tell you, I grew up then. Sixteen-year-old boy from Rochester, New York, how else am I gonna see the world? Paris: Folies Bergère, women, wine. Copenhagen: Clean, really clean. The same with Holland. I brought a camera in this little Dutch town, a Retina 2 — I got

a really good deal because I was the first American in this place. I had a trail of beautiful Dutch kids following me everywhere, hugging me. Little Hans Brinkers. "Chocolate, chocolate!" That was the only English they knew. I was a hero.

I must have taken 20 rolls of film: the kids, their mothers, the houses, the tulips, lots of tulips. I printed the shots back at the base just to see those little Hans Brinkers slowly materialize on Army-issue paper. But I rationed myself; three Hans Brinkers a day, four on bad days.

Five, six.

Twenty.

Ghost Father sits in the chair

Bad days in the darkroom. Those other shots were bad. I let those other shots get to me. Too involved with the subject. Stupid, damn stupid. Too sensitive. Weak. Typical, really typical. Depressing.

Whoa, let's not go down that road.

He falls backwards out of the chair

Light Cue 29: Black out

I PICK UP THE METAL CHAIR and sit down. The theater is silent. It's Monday morning, I'm on my third week here and determined to let the students talk first. A full minute passes.

Another minute.

Nebraskans are Olympians when it comes to silence.

They win. This is a literature class so I say, "Have any of you read…" A short young woman in a red tracksuit sporting a blond bouffant, interrupts, "Did your daddy really kill himself?" I have learned enough to just answer the question, "Yes."

"How old were you?"

"I was eight."

"I'm sorry."

"Thanks." I let the silence sit, resisting the urge to try to talk about theater or literature. Eventually the young woman says, "My daddy died when I was 15. Cancer. He was sick a long time."

"I'm sorry about your father."

"Thanks. Your story made me think of him 'cause he rode a motorcycle. An Indian. An old one, dark red with a leather seat. I miss him."

"I miss my dad, too."

A friend hands the young woman a tissue and we're quiet for awhile. Eventually, a huge guy, who I assume is a lineman on the Cornhuskers, raises his hand and, when I nod to him, he says, "My grandpa was in the war." His bass drawl is from the Deep South. "World War Two. Infantry. He never talks about it, though."

"My dad didn't either."

"Then how'd you get the information for your play?"

"My mom gave me some letters my dad wrote home from Germany and I remembered some things from when I was a kid, like the motorcycle. I made up the rest."

"You can do that, just make stuff up?"

"You can, yes. That's what an artist does. But it's dangerous. My brother hates *Father-Land*. He said I got it wrong about the motorcycle, that daddy was just going to take us up to Rochester, not to California."

"What's the big deal, Rochester or California?"

"My brother's a scientist and we always get in arguments about me telling stories, not sticking to the facts. And, truthfully, I don't think he wanted to see a play about his dad killing himself. Can't blame him, really."

"I used to tell people my grandpa was a war hero, make up stuff about him being a Tuskegee Airman, dogfighting with the Krauts. My mamma would yell at me, telling me not to ever let Grandpa hear that nonsense."

"My grandfather was in the Pacific Theater." A young man stands up. He's wearing a ROTC uniform and glasses with stylish black frames. "He got shrapnel in his leg at Iwo Jima, used to walk with a limp. He'd tell me stories about the war but none of the bloody stuff, just about what they ate and how he and his buddies would go dancing in Okinawa whenever they got shore leave."

More kids talk, some cry. They ask me a few questions but mainly I listen.

Thirty minutes goes by, the class is over, but no one leaves. We're talking about our families and we're talking about art and we're talking about pain and we're laughing together. The theater feels small and cozy.

Eventually the students trickle out. I end up talking to the big lineman until we notice students coming in for the next class. Before he leaves, the big guy gives me a bear hug. "Thank you, man. That was a great class."

Not wanting to jinx it, I do the same scene for the afternoon class and wait just as long for a question. This time it is, "Do you have your dad's photographs from the war?" Again, I just answer the question "yes" and wait for them to start telling their stories. Although I don't get another bear hug, a few of the students come up after class to keep talking and the professor gives a thumbs-up on his way out of the theater.

That evening Katharine takes me out for a dinner at the Thai restaurant and congratulates me on my new approach. I say, "But I'm just sitting there and letting them do all the work."

"Exactly."

CHAPTER TWENTY-EIGHT

PLAYING WITH FIRE

"KIKE!"

"Yes, good one." I write k-i-k-e up on the whiteboard under "hook nose" and "killer of Jesus." In the next column over, we've got "rag head" and "terrorist" and the final column has "redneck" and "white trash."

"Let's get some more."

It's Monday morning, week four of my Nebraska tour, and I'm on to a new project: working with seven students to write and perform a show that celebrates Easter, Passover and Ramadan all at once. We have one performance, Sunday night, and a week to write and rehearse.

The students are sitting on tables and chairs scattered around a small classroom in the basement of a life sciences building. They don't look like a typical UNL class: Zehra is an exchange student from Istanbul, wearing expensive jeans, a stylish black tee and a huge silver necklace. She's our only Muslim. Greta, in an orange skirt and a purple chiffon blouse with puffy sleeves, was raised Catholic in Berlin. The other five are from rural Nebraska, ranging from Matt, a rotund freshman dressed head to toe in red sportswear with "Huskers" bold across his chest, to Penny, a tiny 28-year-old second-generation Mexican-American sophomore in gray slacks, a white shirt and a tie. They are all various shades of Christian. I'm holding down the Jewish corner.

"We need to get the ugliest language, the words that have powered crusades and bombings and gas chambers; we need those words out in the open before we start looking for common ground." Most of the students are nodding, so I go on. "We have to be honest with each other, and ourselves, about the power these words have over our thoughts and feelings. And then we have to forgive each other when we offend. Luckily, we're in Nebraska so we know everything will stay polite..." A couple of the small-town kids make sarcastic remarks about "Nebraska Nice."

"No, no, nice is good. In San Francisco, for all of our tie-dyed grooviness, we like nothing better than a rip-roaring political fight. Not helpful for what we're trying to do here." I point to our lists on the whiteboard. "Our job is to politely talk about really nasty, gnarly, vicious ideas, tell each other stories, write a play from those stories and perform it on Sunday night. Easy." They smile and we spend another hour on our lists, laughing at some words, getting very quiet when a slur hits home. After lunch, we start to teach each other our different rituals.

THE CAST MEMBERS are excited and generous and by Tuesday the show is starting to take shape. By Wednesday, though, I realize I've underestimated the flattening effect of Nebraska Nice — we have settled into a congenial rhythm of "let's share our foods, festivals and folklore." They gently refuse to go deeper.

I push hard the rest of the week but our dress rehearsal on Saturday feels too tame. I had high hopes for this play, too high; you can't make deeply moving political theatre in six days. To be fair, it has some good moments: the cast sings traditional songs, we have a Turkish dance and serve wine to the audience — who doesn't like that? And a food fight, punctuated by racial slurs, adds a little dramatic tension.

Light Cue 1: Full stage warm wash

<u>Zehra</u>

This is my first Easter party. I'm from Turkey and, you know, we don't celebrate Easter, at least my family doesn't. Perhaps the Christians do, but there aren't that many in Turkey. Christians, I mean. We're Muslim. Not with the head covering and all, but... *(she finishes the sentence in Turkish)* I'm so sorry; you don't speak

Turkish, do you?

The Cast

Terrorist, kidnapper, raghead, convenience store owner, jihadi.

Zehra

When I came to Nebraska, people were very interested in my culture. They would always ask, "Do you ride camels?" I live in a city three times the size of Omaha; I don't ride camels. At first, I was really hurt by your ignorance, but then I remembered that I used to think all Nebraskans were real cowboys with big hats, riding horses and roping cows all day. Now I know you ride pickups.

Matt

All I know about Ramadan is that Muslims can't eat during the day. They must get hungry here at UNL with everyone else scarfing on brats and drinking beer. Can they even eat pork? Wait, maybe that's Jews. Maybe both. I don't know. And I don't think they can sing or dance at Ramadan, either. That would be hard for me — not eating and especially not singing. I love music.

The Cast

Racist, selfish, WASP, big mouth, slave-owner, goyim, redneck.

Matt

I used to sing in the choir at my high school. We got our first chance to shine at the Big Eight Conference on Black Student Government in Columbia, Missouri. During the conference we all ate together, all twelve hundred of us. The only other whites there were the wait staff and a handful of other singers. On Friday night, they served steak. Unfortunately, I had to send it back because I'm Catholic; it was during Lent and I couldn't partake of meat on a Friday. Everyone stared at me. "Something's wrong with the white boy. He can't eat meat or something like that."

Greta

I've never been to a Passover before. Actually, I'm told it's called a "Seder." But it must be a lot like Easter. I'm from Germany. We are mostly Christian, some Muslims, not a lot of Jews these days, of course, because of the war.

The Cast

Shylocks, JAPs, bankers, greedy, nerdy cheapskates, Christ killers.

Greta

Many German men died in the war, so afterwards we needed male workers for jobs Germans didn't want to do — hard factory work and other dirty jobs. Turkish men were hired to come over, without their families, as guest workers. They lived in isolated camps, did the dirty work and sent their money home to Turkey. Later, they brought their families over — wives and mothers with covered hair and lots of children, all speaking Turkish.

My neighborhood is mixed — students, workers and Turkish families. Walking home, I see old men sitting outside drinking their Turkish coffee, old women with covered hair doing handicrafts and watching the grandchildren while the parents work at their Turkish restaurants. The Turks keep their shops open late into the night, and on Sundays, even though this isn't really legal in Germany. But I love the atmosphere of my neighborhood and their food is very tasty and cheap. I profit so much from Turks being my neighbors.

Light Cue 2: Crossfade to spotlight on Zehra

CHAPTER TWENTY-NINE

WESTBORO BAPTIST CHURCH

THE EASTER/PASSOVER/RAMADAN show opened and closed last night. After some polite applause, the audience, mainly students with a few faculty members and even folks from town, just sat there. For a moment, I was back in Alaska, where the Yup'ik audiences wait for their favorite acts to do an encore at breakneck speed. As it turned out, this Nebraska audience was waiting to talk; when the cast came out a few minutes later, questions, stories and strong words began to fly at a very un-Nebraska volume.

We'd hit a nerve. The show gave the audience a chance to talk about things they usually avoid. We were there so late that the campus police came by to tell us, politely, to go home.

Maybe we went just deep enough.

Early this morning I got a call from my boss's boss, the dean. "I hear the police came after I left the theater last night. What happened?" I bragged about the post-show energy, how the play elicited exactly the conversations that the university had schlepped me all the way from San Francisco to create. The phone line got quiet.

Finally, the dean said, "I was disappointed in the production values. Theater at such an amateur level makes the department look bad."

Now it was my turn to be quiet, mainly out of shock. Is he serious? Did he expect *West Side Story* from a week of writing and rehearsing with a group of non-writers and non-actors? No, this has nothing to do with form; it has to do with content. Maybe the dean isn't as interested in artists and diversity as he pretends to be. Well, there is nothing much he can do now — we've had our one performance. He can fire me, of course, which would mean I'd get home three weeks early; not the worst outcome.

"You're right, sir. The performances weren't as strong as they needed to be with such a charged subject."

"I'm glad you see it my way."

"I do, I do. I've got to go to Omaha later today but let's meet this evening to put together a budget for me to re-write the piece as a proper play and then stage it, maybe in the fall, with a professional cast. We could even partner with Nebraska Rep to offer more performances."

Silence.

"That's a bit more ambitious than our budget will allow." And the conversation was over.

NOW CHET AND I are in his pickup heading to Omaha on another field trip, albeit a short one. I'm doing a presentation at a high school that Chet assures me is one of the best in town. He parks at the far end of the huge lot and as we walk between cars to get to the school, he says, "There is one thing you should know — the senior class president killed himself last week."

"What? Why didn't we cancel?"

"Because of who the kid is, or was. He transferred here two years ago after getting bullied for being gay in another high school. Apparently he was suicidal back then — if you'd been bullied like that, you would be, too — but somehow he found a place at this school and became the first openly gay class president in Omaha. A great story until he hanged himself. Everyone was shocked."

"That's horrible. So why are we here?"

"This school is all about diversity now, at least about being gay or straight or whatever, and diversity is what you talk about. They're having a big memorial for the kid right after your class so it's a perfect fit."

We go in a side door and walk down a wide, well-lit hallway with a polished tile floor. Chet finds our room, a lecture hall with the seats at a steep incline. The class starts in 10 minutes so I scramble to rearrange my presentation in my mind while writing my name on the whiteboard. There's a burst of voices behind me; I turn around and a half-dozen cheerleaders are walking down the center aisle toward the stage. They look like extras in *American Graffiti*. The leader, medium height, long blonde hair and a mouthful of gum, says, "You the diversity guy from Lincoln?"

"Yes. My name is…"

She puts her palm in my face — "talk to the hand" — and then points to a four-inch piece of rainbow ribbon folded over and pinned to her uniform above her left breast.

"You gonna wear one of these or are you a fraud?"

The other cheerleaders all point to their ribbons in unison. I resist the urge to applaud and say, "I'd be honored to wear a rainbow ribbon."

The leader snaps her fingers; a tall girl with red hair pulls a large spool of ribbon from somewhere in her uniform; the girl next to her pulls out a pinking shears and cuts a piece of ribbon on the bias. The leader is holding a safety pin, which she expertly threads through the ribbon and attaches to my shirt pocket in one smooth move.

"OK, then. Whatcha gonna talk to us about?"

Luckily, the rest of the class comes in before I have to answer and the cheerleaders sit down in the front row. They cross their legs and pop their gum. The seats fill up and I notice that most kids are wearing rainbow ribbons. My whole lesson plan and performance is out the window. Instead, I ask them about the young man, about how he was elected class president and about the memorial service. Kids tell stories, cry; some are silent, most are mad.

"Fucking Fred Phelps said he's coming to picket the memorial service today."

I ask, "Who is Fred Phelps?"

"Reverend Fred 'God Hates Fags' Phelps? Of the Westboro Baptist church? Never heard of him? Wow, where've you been?

"Phelps brings his whole family, even little kids, to picket *funerals*. How low is that?"

"I'm Christian, right? Most of us are Christian but not *his* kind of Christian."

The head cheerleader stands up and turns to the class. "He's not picketing our memorial, is he?" The kids shout "No!" and "Damn straight!"

I get them calmed down a little and we hear a few more stories about the class president before the bell rings. The kids bolt up the stairs and out the door, heading, I assume, to the memorial. We follow them out. In the hall, I ask Chet, "Did you know about this guy Phelps?"

"There was something in the paper about him maybe coming."

"And you didn't mention it to me?"

"I wanted to see you in action, see how you'd handle it. Damn, you're good."

I walk a little faster. Chet catches up, "Don't worry, I did some research and found out that Phelps was a civil rights lawyer before he started his 'God Hates Fags' crap. Even got an award from the NAACP. Crazy, huh?" I keep walking. "I know you like things complex, like the German lady who's all into Turkish restaurants. 'No easy answers.' I was ready to give you the dirt on Phelps if things got rough with the kids."

"Thanks, Chet. You're a saint."

At least a thousand students, plus teachers and staff, are standing on the huge, sloping lawn in front of the school. A voice is coming through the loudspeakers, probably the principal, talking about loss and grief and acceptance. Now a different voice is talking, a girl, telling a story we just heard in class. Students around us are openly sobbing. Now the head cheerleader is doing her job: leading a cheer. Kids are screaming through their tears. I look for picket signs but it seems Reverend Fred Phelps didn't show. He must have gotten wind of the cheerleaders and decided he was outmatched. Smart man.

Brenda Thurston's throat is sore from cheering. Her mom makes her tea with honey and lemon, which she takes to her room. The house rule is "food and drinks in the kitchen only" but her mom doesn't say anything; she knows it's been a tough day. Danny's dead.

All the rainbow ribbons and marching around and leading cheers have kept Brenda from thinking those words.

Danny is dead.

Brenda shakes her head hard, trying to keep an image of Danny hanging in his closet from creeping in behind her eyes. It doesn't work. She sobs, taking big gasping breaths between quiet tears.

Her mother comes in and sits by her little girl, her perfect cheerleader now crumpled on her bed looking frail and tiny. She can't think of anything to say. Mothers are supposed to know what to say but she's got nothing.

"It'll be OK." Well, no, it won't be OK. The boy is dead.

"Tomorrow is another day." So what, another day to cry and feel guilty?

She sits and strokes her daughter's hair. Brenda was Danny's friend, right from the start, the odd couple of Omaha North, the Cheerleader and the Queer. At first, girls were cruel, calling Brenda "fag hag" and "lesbo," which only made Brenda mad — she'd always been stubborn that way. But as Danny made friends and become popular and then, amazingly, got voted class president, Brenda pulled away. They're kids; this happens. They were an odd pair to begin with. Now there is more than enough guilt to go around.

CHAPTER THIRTY

A CROSS IS BURNING

BACK IN MY APARTMENT, before going to bed, I call my fiancée. We talk about the wedding, which is less than five months away: who's not coming, who we can now invite, how much the cake will cost, when we will meet with the rabbi. As we're about to hang up, she says, "Wait, you got a call from Alaska today. Someone named Stephanie says she's got a job for you next January. January in Alaska? A little too cold for me but here's the number if you're interested."

With the time difference, I reach Stephanie as she's making dinner. We haven't talked in three years, since she booked Tina and me on a tour of one-night stands in 16 Alaskan towns, but she's not the type to chitchat. "Got a contract for a month-long residency in St. Michael. Solo, just you this time. Next January. Interested?"

I say I might be. We talk about St. Michael and the fee and I promise to give her a firm answer in a couple of weeks. Going to work for Stephanie out on the tundra — again — seems like a step backward. Been there, done that. But no one is clamoring to book *Father-Land* on Broadway, or in Pocatello or anywhere else for that matter.

My fiancée and I have a deal: After the wedding, I'm going to look for more work at home and tour less. I'm fine with that; life as a Road Warrior is wearing thin after 16 years of touring. I'm yearning for family and a community to live in, not just visit. I can write plays from home, if anyone will pay me for them. But in the meantime, performing and teaching are what will pay my share of the bills. And I still feel a twinge when I think of Alaska, a twinge of regret that, after all these trips, I still haven't found a way to make a truly Eskimo circus.

9:37 AM. NO ALARM. Stay in bed. It's Tuesday, I worked through the weekend so this is my day off.

I start my last big project here at UNL tomorrow — creating another show, this time with the teachers' college. I have three weeks, an eternity compared to the last one, with a class of folks who are already student-teaching. Most of them will have their own classrooms next year so they are hungry for curriculum ideas. Making this play will be more about "the artistic process" than the theme of the piece, more of the art part of my title and less about diversity. That's just as well since I haven't got a clue what the theme might be.

Eventually I get dressed and I treat myself to breakfast at The Mill, my uncle's café. The coffee is so good I catch myself moaning out loud. There's a copy of the Daily Nebraskan on a table near me and I peek at the headline: "Cross Burning at Frat House, University Orders Investigation."

Cross burning?

I grab the paper and read the article. It seems that Sigma Chi burned a cross last week as part of a secret fraternity ritual and somehow the word got out. The secretary of state says he doesn't understand the problem, that they've been burning crosses at Sigma Chi every year since he was a student. "It has something to do with Emperor Constantine." What planet is he on?

Then they quote the Interfraternity Council president: "I just think that if this skit was really terrible and demeaning, things would have been taken care of a long time ago. From now on, I will encourage UNL fraternities to conduct their rituals in private so no one can witness the events." I see — *private* cross burnings are fine. How about private lynchings?

Way down below the fold, the reporter quotes someone from the African Student Association saying that maybe a burning cross has meaning beyond a Roman emperor. Maybe?!

I *have* to use this for my play with the student teachers. I have to. My next three weeks just got a lot more interesting; a shitload of gnarly mixed in with the art.

ON THE FIRST DAY of rehearsal, 22 of us sit on folding chairs, just barely fitting in the long, thin classroom we've been assigned. Looking around, I can't imagine any of them standing in front of a room teaching; they all look too young. Maybe I'm too old.

Unlike my previous cast, these folks did not choose this project — it is an assignment. Some make it clear with their body language and monosyllabic responses that they would rather be anywhere else. I want to get right to the tough stuff: institutional racism, hate symbols, personal bias. They want to go home.

That first day we mainly tell stories to get to know each other. On Day 2, I introduce the theme and we start to explore the world of symbols, including hate symbols. The room gets tense; feelings get hurt. I invent the "offensive tick" — if someone says something offensive, instead of arguing or interrupting, anyone can make a tick mark in the air with one finger, a little half quote. My promise is that we will get back to those offensive moments and discuss them before the rehearsal is over.

We've only used the "offensive tick" once or twice, when someone says something purposefully outrageous; Nebraska Nice kicks in whenever folks get too hot.

On Friday, we're scheduled to go until 8 pm. At 6:30, I mention that I am planning to excuse them an hour early, "since you are all students and I'm sure you've got parties to go to tonight." A dozen fingers make a dozen tick marks. I must have looked completely puzzled since they all laugh.

"So every student parties on Friday nights?"

"Maybe we want to spend our Friday night rehearsing. Did you think of that?"

"You have a lot of personal bias about us, don't you?"

From then on, the "offensive tick" and Nebraska Nice were our safety valves, letting us get very real, very raw, without splintering into hostile camps. But the day before our only performance, tempers flare and a few folks leave rehearsal early, slamming the door behind them. Everyone else is shaken and the class ends with the real possibility of having to cancel the show.

But the next afternoon, all 21 of them are at the theater on time to set up our stage and rehearse. No one mentions the door-slamming. I set a few simple lighting cues with the stage manager and call "places."

The dress rehearsal is a bumbling mess of mumbled lines, missed cues, awkward pauses and prairie-flat line readings. It goes so slowly that I have to stop the play a few pages before the end to let the audience into the theater. I pray the cast gets it together before we start, since the seats are filling fast and folks are lined up out the door.

Light Cue 1: Spotlight on sign stage left, "All Tangled Up"

Light Cue 2: PHYSICAL CUE — Ringmaster enters, pan Spotlight to him

<u>Ringmaster</u>

Ladies and gentlemen, faculty and students, liberals and conservatives, welcome to the center ring. You have seen the articles, the debates, the passions and accusations after the cross burning at Sigma Chi.

Now I call your attention to these 21 teachers-to-be. Look closer. You will see someone who helped burn the cross and someone who led protests against it, someone who recently came to this country and folks whose families have been here for generations, people who feel deeply on all sides of this issue and others who would shrug it off. I need not insult your intelligence by saying "we've solved this one." That cross burns us all like a brand.

The cross — why did they burn it? Who has the right to say what it means? Did the cross burners really believe their "skit was an innocent skit?" Imagine their classmates and the shadow that fire casts on their lives.

<u>Edward</u>

I called Big Grandma Edna to ask her a few questions for this play. She said she never had any experience with racism, really. My Big Grandma Edna was one of those young women who first wore dark lipstick. She and her friends would hike up their dresses and go out dancing to ragtime music. She was a wild woman. She said she had never even seen "one of them" until she and my grandpa moved from South Dakota to California.

Sandy

I was sleeping one night in our house in North Omaha when I was startled awake by tapping noises coming from the sun porch next to my room. I'd always had nightmares about someone breaking into my room through the sun porch at night.

Amazing. I can hear the actors, even all the way in the back, and they sound like real human beings, not robots.

Ringmaster

Why would anyone burn a cross?

Klansman

We light the cross with fire to signify that Jesus Christ is the light of the world. Where the Holy Light shall shine, there will be dispelled evil, darkness, gloom and despair. The Light of Truth dispels ignorance and superstition as fire purifies gold, but destroys wood. Who can look upon this sublime symbol without being inspired with a Holy desire to be a better person?

Davey

He had swastika tattoos on his arms, head bald and clean-shaven. We met in a dark bar at lunchtime, his call. There were only a couple of old guys on stools downing beers. We sat in a booth. I needed this interview for a good perspective on the cross burning. I asked him what he thought of the Sigma Chi ritual. He chuckled and said:

Bald Guy

Those frat boys don't know nothing about racial gestures or racism. Amateurs. They burned the cross with cotton tips to make a small fire, for appearances only; if real racists had done it, it would have been a huge cross, a four-alarm fire and chanting by all the skins.

Davey

He thought that if there was any racism in the Sigma Chi ritual, it might be in the Confederate Army outfits the students wore, but he doubted it. Suddenly, he bowed his head, stuck his arm out with his fist clenched, and chanted:

Bald Guy

We, the brothers of the world, do not allow this world to be taken by the niggers, Jews and the rest of this nation. Kill the niggers, Kill the Jews, Burn the rest. White is the way; we are a dying breed and need not let the monkeys steal our jobs or lives.

Davey

He stopped. I looked around but no one in the bar seemed to notice or care.

Bald Guy

If those frat boys were for real, that's what they would have chanted.

Davey

I quickly thanked him, stood up and speed walked to the door. He started pounding his fist on the table, yelling:

<u>Bald Guy</u>
They all must die! They all must die!

<u>Davey</u>
I ran to my car.

<u>Ringmaster</u>
Can we say the n-word, even in this context?

The audience isn't walking out. Yet. We're packed into this small chapel-cum-theater, sitting on hard wooden benches with the heaters cranked up, watching a show that has got something to really piss off everybody here.

<u>Edward</u>
I asked if Big Grandma Edna if she had anything to say about the first time she saw a black person. She said "not really," then yelled to my grandpa, "George, do you have anything to say about the first time you saw a nigger?" My grandpa just said "No." I didn't say anything. I was stunned. These are my grandparents. I love them. How could they talk like that?

<u>Ringmaster</u>
Can we say the n-word in this context?

<u>Sandy</u>
The tapping kept going. I was terrified. I decided to call my sister. You see, we shared the same room, but we hated each other and separated the room with a wall of dressers so I didn't have to see her. I called to her over the dressers, whisper-yelling since I didn't want whoever was breaking in to know I was awake.

<u>Huong</u>
When I was a little girl, my family came to Lincoln.

There were many Vietnamese people who already lived here. They told us the new things we needed to know about Americans.

One: Black people are violent, lazy and sex-aggressive. They like to live on food stamps and welfare.

Two: Hispanics are poor.

Three: White people, who are descended from Germany or Russia, are mean, cold-blooded jerks.

Four: Asian people, especially Vietnamese, don't like to pay income taxes so many of them cheat the IRS.

Since then I have learned that these are stereotypes. Now it is hard for me to say them, even right now, to you.

<u>Sandy</u>
First thing in the morning I told my sister about the tapping. We went together to the sun porch and saw a little sparrow, trapped inside. It was tapping on the window to get out. We watched as it banged its beak on the pane, over and over again, adding more and more blood to the red-streaked glass.

Huong, who had begged me to cut her section, stood tall and delivered; Sandy told her trapped bird story like it was Edgar Allen Poe. The audience isn't scaring the actors; it's giving them a reason to be brave — a living, breathing community to talk to from their hearts.

The audience does scare me — mullets, afros, shaved scalps and nose rings; spiderweb and swastika tattoos; letter shirts and leather, tweeds and tees; black, white, Asian and Latino, even some folks I recognize from the Omaha Nation. It's getting sweaty in here already and we still have a long way to go.

CHAPTER THIRTY-ONE

GETTING OUT OF DODGE

"...emergency exits...life preservers...seat belts...sit back and relax..."

I'M ON THE RED-EYE heading home. Two hours ago, Chet dragged me out of the post-show discussion-turned-shouting match; the audience was not shy about telling us which parts of the play offended them most and why. *All Tangled Up* put the kibosh on Nebraska Nice.

The campus police were arriving as Chet was throwing my luggage into the back of his pickup. "Well good, the party's gonna break up soon so we won't be missing much of the fun."

The plane gets airborne, the wheels tuck into the fuselage and I finally feel my shoulders ease away from my ears. I've never been happier to be in a middle seat in the back row of a 727.

The play was designed to stir things up; a mix of stories, quotes and metaphors guaranteed to create friction. I wanted *All Tangled Up* to say what wasn't being said, to start the conversations that would be hard but might, eventually, defuse some of the anger. I tried to do what Anna Deavere Smith did with *Fires in the Mirror,* a play stitched together from interviews with dozens of people after an Orthodox Jewish driver killed a 7-year-old Caribbean-American boy and their already-tense Crown Heights neighborhood exploded. Smith's play let us meet the human beings, hear about their lives and eventually make it almost impossible for us to pass absolute judgment.

Lincoln didn't explode but our play might have created more anger than it defused. I'll never know. The conversations about *All Tangled Up* over the next few weeks — in classes, on the streets and in the Daily Nebraskan — will tell. I won't be there. I'll be home.

One thing that I am sure of: Making and performing *All Tangled Up* changed the 21 student teachers-turned-writers-and-actors. They will be different people, and better teachers, because of the time we spent together. I will be too.

"Beverage?"

I order a ginger ale. I never drink ginger ale below 30,000 feet; it just goes with flying.

"Peanuts or pretzels?"

Peanuts just go with ginger ale, so that's a no-brainer.

Sipping my Canada Dry, popping some peanuts, my nerves start to un-jangle. I close my eyes and let my mind drift, inevitably, home to San Francisco.

I'm getting married in four months. That hasn't sunk in.

"Getting hitched." "Tying the knot." "Jumping the broom." "Putting on the ball and chain." Is it possible to get married without becoming a cliché?

I never thought I'd be a husband; that's just not what Road Warriors do. Most of my friends are single and most who aren't don't have kids. Road Warriors go wherever the work is, cutting ties and leaving broken hearts behind. But after a while there are precious few ties to cut and you're stuck with a hard, achy heart.

This wedding is what I want and my fiancée is the woman I love. I'm sure of that. I will promise to spend the rest of my life with her, loudly and without hesitation. Where I get queasy is imagining myself as a husband and then, in a year or so, as a father. Forever. I've been a juggler, a clown, an actor, a teacher and a would-be playwright; that's what I know how to do. I can juggle five clubs but I can't fix a toilet or find a babysitter or tell my wife what makes me happy or scared. I've made a career for myself in a tough field by exploiting a flair for throwing things. How does that help me now?

"More peanuts?"

I put a couple of bags of nuts into my carry-on; thank-you gifts to my fiancée for picking me up at SFO.

Before I left for Lincoln we tried on the wedding rings. I've never worn rings and it felt like a lug nut on my finger. Juggling is almost impossible with it on, which is too depressingly metaphoric. Then we went house hunting in a suburb of San Francisco and every block featured a seemingly well-staged tableau of men washing cars and mowing lawns. I don't wash cars and I don't mow lawns! "Do any of you guys pass seven clubs? Shakespeare, anyone? Flip-flops?"

"Excuse me, mind if I get out?"

The woman in the window seat shimmies out as the guy on the aisle and I dutifully stand up. We wait while she goes to the bathroom, stretching our legs and carefully not chatting — no one wants to risk listening to someone else's problems for three hours. The woman comes back, we settle in, I work on Hemispheres magazine's crossword, getting a couple of words short of a full grid before my eyes close.

> "…collect any remaining service items. We will be landing in San Francisco in approximately 30 minutes."

Wow, I actually slept. Sweet. I collect my stuff, peek past the woman in the window seat to catch a glimpse of some snowcaps and settle in for the hardest stretch, the last half hour before we hit the runway.

My mind turns to work. The rest of my year is a freelancer's dream — solid, paid gigs through to New Year's Day. Add on the Alaska trip and I'll be making regular money straight through February next year. What is less thrilling is that none of these jobs has anything to do with *Father-Land* or a commission for a new play. I may be a playwright in Nebraska, but in the rest of the world I'm a clown.

This summer I've got Bottom in a circus production of *A Midsummer Night's Dream* in a local theater. My old clown partner Tina will be playing Puck. After the wedding and a honeymoon to British Columbia, I'll do a stint teaching commedia dell'arte at the San Francisco equivalent of the *Fame* high school, followed by a return trip to Yosemite National Park in December. I'll play the Jester again in the Bracebridge Dinner, a four-hour show featuring 30 opera singers, some supernumeraries, great food and me. There is nothing quite like walking to work through the snow, across the valley from Half Dome and within misting range of

Yosemite Falls, dressed in jester's motley and cap, carrying a bauble and wearing Sorel boots over my tights.

Last year my fiancée and I shared a very romantic little cabin for the two-week run; I proposed to her on the last day. It was raining as we drove out of the park and the next morning we read in the papers that the Merced River had flooded. All the cabins, including ours, washed away in the night. I'm hoping that the romance of Yosemite didn't wash away with the cabin.

> "…for those of you who live in the San Francisco Bay Area, welcome home."

ACT III

FROZEN IN TIME

St. Michael, Alaska
Winter 1996

CHAPTER THIRTY-TWO

FLY BY NIGHT CLUB

"...for those of you flying on Alaska Airlines flight 97,
boarding will be delayed due to weather in Anchorage."

DEPENDING ON HOW LONG we wait here at SFO, I might miss my connecting flight. It's January, I'm going to Alaska so I gave myself an extra day to get to St. Michael.

The truth is I'm hoping to miss my second flight and have tonight off in Anchorage. I need time to get back into Road Warrior mode. Since the wedding, my wife and I haven't had a night apart and it's been heaven. All the sweetness with only the tiniest taste of the claustrophobia I used to think was the dominant flavor of marriage. The hotel room in Yosemite Lodge wasn't as romantic as our cabin last year, but the park was so beautiful it didn't matter — a foot of soft snow covering everything; 30-degree days and crisp, clear nights; elk and coyotes wandering the meadows with huge hawks gliding overhead. And those amazing waterfalls, frozen solid. If I hadn't been off doing shows most of the time, it would have been a second honeymoon.

We've only been home a week and now I'll be gone for a month, the first test of time apart. When I used to go up to Alaska, I left without anyone pulling on my heart from home. Granted, Tina was with me on my first tundra trip, but that fell apart before we got back to the Bay Area and we've been on platonic clown partner status ever since. Now I just want to be home with my wife, not sitting at a crowded gate at SFO.

If I get stuck in Anchorage, I can try to cure my homesickness by going to the Fly by Night Club, a jazz joint with spam in every dish on the menu. They have a huge selection of beers and a $3 fine if you're stupid enough to order a Bud. Their motto — "We're Turning Rudeness and Bad Taste into the Fun Things They Used to Be!" A Road Warrior joint if there ever was one.

The same iconic Eskimo is staring at me from the tail of the Alaska Airlines plane. I wish Tina was flying with me; we always talked about that logo, how it was an Eskimo seen through gussak eyes. Now that I'm married, though, it might be unseemly to spend a month with Tina in a little village 125 miles south of Nome. This is a solo trip, just me and the frozen north, one last chance to make a show that is a circus seen through Yup'ik eyes.

> "Flight 97 to Anchorage will be delayed for another 30 minutes. Please don't leave the waiting area; weather conditions in Alaska are unpredictable so we may need to board quickly to take advantage of a sudden clearing in Anchorage."

Looks like I'll get to visit the Fly by Night Club tonight. Luckily I'm traveling light, just my suitcase and a carry-on since Stephanie shipped 17 bags of circus equipment directly to St. Michael last week.

To avoid wallowing in homesickness before I even board the plane, I pull a red paper file folder out of my bag and start to read through the letters from Stephanie. Looks like I'm staying in the spare bedroom at the principal's house, a huge improvement over gym floors and storerooms. And the principal has been in St. Michael for nearly a decade so he's clearly committed to the school and can help me navigate the politics of the village. All good. I put the folder away.

Four weeks — a whole month — in a village of 400 people. It feels strange looking at the old Eskimo on the tail of the plane and not wanting to go north, even feeling scared that I'm going far away and for so long. What if something happens to me up there? Worse, what if something happens to my wife? Or what if she decides it's better having me gone? What if, what if, what if...

"Last call for Flight 97 to Anchorage. We are boarding all rows. The gate will close in 5 minutes."

THE FLY BY NIGHT CLUB was as good as I remembered: spam pizza, beer brewed in Homer, and a swinging trio out of Juneau; even danced with a few locals (I left by 10, alone, in case you were getting nervous).

As I walk into the overheated hotel lobby, a grizzly old-timer in overalls recognizes me, "Hey, you're one of the juggling guys used to work the State Fair, right? From Frisco." Turns out Chuck, who is now a roofer living up near Fairbanks, was a rodeo clown back in the day.

"They called me Chuckles. Had to give up clowning though." He unsnaps the bib of his overalls and pulls up his denim shirt; there is a scar on his stomach the size and shape of a small plate. He turns around and there's a smaller circle on his back "where the bull's horn came out."

We go into the hotel bar for a beer.

Chuck is on his way home after three months in the "big city" working on the roof of a new performing arts center. The center's architect, not a local, insisted on an intricate combination of slopes that, predictably, created an avalanche after the first good snow. The patrons waiting in the ticket line got buried, so Chuck and a dozen other Alaskan roofers have been making good money putting in heating units in the roof to melt snow on contact. "Damn roof'll look like it's in Florida, year-round. I don't even want to think about their electric bill." Chuck rolls his eyes and downs his beer. "Glad I got a wood stove."

When Chuck moves on to tequila, I head up to my room. Thinking about an outsider designing a roof in Alaska that can't get snowed on blows my mind. Why make something here that doesn't belong here? How clueless. How arrogant. How much is that like teaching juggling and clowning to people who have never seen a circus, will never see a circus, and can never get a job in a circus?

CHAPTER THIRTY-THREE

PRINCIPALS

AFTER A FEW HOURS OF SLEEP, I get up in time to catch the early flight to St. Michael. Now I'm folded into a seat on a Twin Otter looking out the window at nothing but flat and white, flying northwest to the shore of Norton Sound. We're already passed the Kuskokwim, according to the pilot, and should be crossing the Yukon soon.

With a whole month in one village I can start slowly; this first week I'll just work circus skills, get to know St. Michael, talk with the Yup'ik language teacher to find some traditional stories we can use in the show — lay the groundwork. Next week I will start to use some of the techniques I developed in Nebraska to make a show that has personal stories, traditional stories and some music, dance and circus. A Yup'ik circus, custom-made for St. Michael.

The Twin Otter lands, we wait for both propellers to get tethered and then deplane down a portable staircase. Two other folks get out with me, a tall Asian man in his early 50s and a bald, burly state trooper. I find my suitcase and walk to the school.

The gym is big and looks new, with bleachers that pull out of the walls to seat maybe 300 folks. My pile of equipment looks small sitting in a corner near the storeroom but it's all there — stilts, juggling stuff, rolla bolla, peacock feathers, makeup and costumes. We used to have a unicycle but Tina and I gave it to Barnsie on our first tour and Stephanie never replaced it.

It's Sunday afternoon and the school is quiet. The principal's office is empty so I go back to the gym, get out a basketball and shoot a few free throws. The tall guy from the flight comes in and joins me. "Play a little one-on-one?" I'm not dressed for it but I can't resist. The guy's named is Kurt Takayama; he's faster than me with a good drive to his right, a 50/50 jump shot and solid defense outside of the paint. I've got 30 pounds on him so I dominate inside. He must be new here too, since he's losing his dribble off the frost heaves almost as much as I am.

21—18, me. We're both soaked and bent over at the waist.

"Nice game. I guess the juggling helps you shoot with either hand." I look up quickly and he laughs, "Read your bio. Impressive." I'm about to ask how he happened to have my bio when he says, "I'm the new principal. They didn't tell you? Chris had some issues down in Florida, didn't make it back from Christmas break, so they asked me to finish out the school year. I was just visiting my family in Seattle for the weekend."

"OK. Am I still staying at your place? I was supposed to stay with Chris."

"Absolutely. I got the guest room all ready, brought up a couple of steaks from Seattle — 100 percent fresh beef, not frozen salmon steaks. You eat meat, I hope."

I confirm my omnivore-ness and then ask what he meant by "Chris had some issues."

"Let's get your stuff over to the house before it gets dark and then we can talk."

ONCE I'M ENSCONCED in the spare bedroom in Kurt's neat three-room house, we sit down at the kitchen table with cappuccinos pulled from the De'Longhi he got for Christmas. "You are one of the reasons I let them drag me out of retirement. My wife and kids aren't thrilled but it's only until summer and they're paying me real well. I keep telling my wife, 'When's the next time I'll get to work with a clown?'"

I take the compliment graciously and make some happy noises about the coffee before getting back to the question of why I'm having this conversation with Kurt instead of Chris.

"Chris went home to Florida for the break and managed to get into a bit of trouble. He's in jail now for possession, cocaine I think, and may be facing some charges having to do with the girl he was with. Chris is a big guy with big appetites but he's always kept it together up here.

Guess his vacations are another story. Shame, too, 'cause Chris is a good principal and was really good for St. Michael, which is saying a lot. This all stays between us, OK?"

I nod my head and take another sip. Cocaine and what, sexual abuse? pimping? statutory rape? And this is a *good* principal. I look at Kurt and remember the state trooper who got off the plane with us. "Is the trooper here about Chris?"

"No, no. That mess is all down in Florida. The trooper is out for a day to talk with a couple of folks in town."

I wait for Kurt to tell me what the trooper will be talking *about* but he just sips and smiles. Kurt looks too young to be retired. He's a handsome guy with straight black hair and Asian features that make him look more like the rest of St. Michael than, say, I do. I imagine he'll be a better roommate than Cokehead Chris and I'm pretty sure I'm going to like working with him, but this game of 20 Questions is getting old.

I outwait my host. "A girl accused someone of molesting her." He raises his hands, palms toward me, "No one in the village believes her; they say she's just trying to get attention. The guy she accused is a good guy, very popular here, does a lot for the village. My guess is the trooper will find out it's not exactly how the girl is saying it is and he'll wrap things up without much trouble."

Another "good guy," like Cokehead Chris? I'm beginning to question Kurt's judgment. I decide not to ask about this alleged child molester.

What have I gotten myself into? Why didn't Stephanie warn me about this place? It reminds me of Mountain Village on my first tour, where a student had taken a potshot at a teacher the day before we arrived. At the time everyone said it was about religion, but now I wonder if there was something else going on between Tim Colbert and the kid. I excuse myself to go down to the store and phone home.

CHAPTER THIRTY-FOUR

OUT IN THE COLD

IT'S FRIDAY AFTER SCHOOL and I'm stashing equipment. The students didn't get excited about circus this week. They haven't warmed to me much, either. Maybe it's the shock of losing their longtime principal, and the rumors flying around about why he's gone. Kurt is still working hard to win their trust — standing at the door every morning to greet each kid by name, asking about relatives, dropping in to observe classes. I'm a big white guy who came out of nowhere; in some of their minds I might be replacing the big white guy they'd all loved and trusted for a decade. "What did you do to Principal Chris? Why are you here instead of him?"

Maybe I just need a little more time. Maybe I'm rusty at this Alaska gig — it's been a few years. Maybe my solo clown show on Monday night wasn't as good as the duets Tina and I used to do. Maybe I want to be writing plays instead of freezing my ass off on the tundra again. Maybe I want to stop trying to be the great white circus savior, like at the Omaha Nation School. Maybe I'm still waiting for the state troopers to arrest someone or for a kid to shoot a teacher. Maybe I miss my wife.

I definitely miss my wife. I want to be home, sleeping in our bed, with her. Or lazing around looking out at the snow falling on Half Dome. I'd better not go down that road — I've still got three more weeks up here.

It hasn't been all bad. The high school kids are learning to juggle and the teachers, a number of whom are Eskimos, are excited to work with me. They like the idea of a Yup'ik circus, even though most folks here speak only English. The Yup'ik language teacher is searching for traditional tales that don't involve too much blood and guts; a lot of the stories she's finding sound like the original Brothers Grimm or the Old Testament. The custodian, Nick Wassilie, is a gregarious version of John McGinty in Eek. Unfortunately he doesn't know the old stories, doesn't speak much Yup'ik, but he's been helping me with everything from putting down mats to keeping the kids focused.

Sliding the bundles of stilts on top of the duffels in the back of the storeroom, I'm starting to feel a little better. I try to pile on the evidence before I start getting homesick again: I only had a day at the Omaha Nation School and I've got a month here; the kids will start trusting me soon. The state trooper left on Tuesday without arresting anyone so maybe that girl *was* just trying to get some attention. The show we make in three weeks could be good, if some of the techniques that worked in Nebraska work up here.

Done packing, time to phone home. My wife's gotten an earful of moaning and groaning every call; now I'm heading down to the store to listen to her life for a change. If I can keep my mouth shut.

I'M SITTING AT KURT'S KITCHEN table after my call home, eating a juicy rare burger with homemade coleslaw; Kurt's in a talking mood. I grill him on the personalities of the different classes, what circus acts he thinks they'll be good at and what stories might click with them. When we get to the third graders, Kurt gets quiet. In class, I've noticed that their noses are runny and they're pretty listless. After some hemming and hawing, Kurt tells me the entire grade is brain damaged from sniffing gasoline.

I put my half-eaten burger down and stare at him.

Kurt goes on to catalog some of the other poisons used in the village: Sterno and vanilla extract, "Friday beer," cough syrup and narcotics that mysteriously show up from time to time. He seems to take this in stride — he's lived in tundra villages for most of his working life, raised his kids in Unalakleet, 70 miles northeast of here. He's seen the collateral damage of the making of modern Alaska. He clearly cares about these kids but he's not shocked that they're sniffing gasoline before they're reading chapter books. I take a sip of water to keep the burger down.

"The whole third grade? I know there's substance abuse here but that's over the top. This village is cursed."

"St. Michael has had it rough, you're right. Rumor has it that the local priest back in the '60s did some of the damage."

"By 'damage' you mean, like, abusing kids?"

"It's just a rumor. No one will talk about it directly, just some vague stories and hints." And he changes the subject back to cartwheels and juggling and what the fourth graders might like.

THE NEXT MORNING Kurt invites me on a snowmobile trip to the neighboring village of Stebbins for a potlatch. "I've got some gifts for the principal's family from my wife — we've known them for years — and you can get a taste of a real Norton Sound potlatch. Lots of dancing."

It's a beautiful day, sunny and above zero. We pack a sled with wrapped gifts, some pots of food that Kurt cooked and a generator he's loaning to the Stebbins school. I bundle up in the same winter gear I bought for my first tundra trip almost two decades ago, with the addition of some long underwear made of a fancy new fabric. I've anchored the wolf tail to the nape of my hood with elastic so it doesn't blow in my face; a little less cool and a lot more comfortable. I guess I'm getting old. I ride behind Kurt on the snow machine the way a biker chick rides a chopper, carefully keeping Kurt's head between the wind and my nose.

We get to Stebbins around noon, unload the sled and walk into the gym. The dancing is already going strong. A row of six drummers sit on folding chairs under the basketball hoop; each drummer holds the handle of a flat white drumhead, a yard in diameter, and hits it with a thin stick. The rhythms are played in unison while the drummers chant. There are two more men near the foul line kneeling, Zen meditation style. They have a dance fan in each hand made of six stiff feathers attached to a wooden base that slides onto their fingers like brass knuckles. Between the male dancers and the drummers is a row of five women, standing and holding fans made of soft caribou beard attached to smaller handles with two finger holes. The dancers make staccato movements right on the beat, the men's fans stabbing the air and the women's waving.

The place is packed. Kurt and I find seats way up in the bleachers on the far side. He shouts in my ear, "Each dance tells a story, although I don't know this one." Some of the movements look like rowing or shooting an arrow; others seem abstract.

We watch the dancing for five hours. The rhythms change slightly and the drummers speed up whenever the audience demands an encore. Some old dancers sit on chairs instead of on their thighs, and sometimes a kid joins in with half-sized dance fans. Other than that, the dance goes on and on like the flat, white tundra. My mind turns to mush.

The rest of the audience is loving it, laughing at jokes I don't get, cheering their favorite dancers, eating little picnics they've packed and playing with the kids who are running around everywhere. Kurt's having fun too, hugging old friends, leading the cheers for his favorite dancers and snacking on finger-fulls of *akutaq*. I'm starving.

The gym gets quiet and I perk up. A woman is walking out of the bleachers wearing a simple yellow *kusbuk* and a big black beard. A titter goes through the crowd as the woman kneels and holds up two stiff feathered fans. A few men get ready to dance on either side of her.

The drums start, the woman dances and her beard bobs up and down to the music. The audience roars and cheers. It's a drag king show. I'm surprised — my image of traditional Yup'ik entertainment is clearly too limited — and I start to wonder about the beard. Most Eskimo men don't grow beards and those who do have wispy ones, not the mountain-man hair glued to this woman's chin. Why is a beard her male signifier of choice? Then again, what else could she have used? Most of the clothing up here is unisex. She's also got the male fans and is dancing in the men's style. The beard works.

The audience makes her dance again and again until the drummers are going too fast for her to keep up. When she walks back into the bleachers, folks cheer and then start moving around. The dancing is over.

"Let's help get the food set up." Kurt leads me to the walk-in fridge and we start taking out plastic-wrap covered plates full of fish and marine mammal meat, bowls of frozen berries, stinkheads and *akutaq*. One plate has cubes of what looks like striated marble. Kurt sees my quizzical expression. "That's *muktuk*. Beluga blubber. Kids up here love it. You chew it like gum." He pulls back the plastic, hands me a piece and I pop it in my mouth. The texture is gum-like, the flavor is subtle and not pleasant —– the unmistakable marine mammal musk. I chew until my jaw aches. A whale hair gets caught between my teeth and I spit the blubber into a napkin. Subtly. Kurt winks at me and says, "You should really leave the rest of the *muktuk* for the kids." I don't argue.

Kurt is visiting friends while I eat salmon and berries off a paper plate and stare at all the beautiful *kusbuks* and fancy sealskin boots in the gym. The heater is blasting and a couple hundred folks are sweating, so after eating I walk down the hall and out the front door to get some air. It's dark, of course, and the wind is howling. The temperature has dropped a lot since we arrived. I wonder when Kurt's planning to head back to St. Michael.

AS IT TURNS OUT, there is no trip home from Stebbins tonight, as we've caught the leading edge of a big storm off the Bering Sea. About 50 of us spend the night in old sleeping bags rolled out on wrestling mats scattered around the gym. In the morning, Kurt and I help make breakfast: leftovers with spam, pilot bread and powdered eggs for everyone. By the time we get cleaned up, the sun is out and the wind is down.

"Betty Wassilie, Nick's mom, needs a ride back to St. Michael. You don't mind sitting on the sled, do you?" I've ridden in sleds around villages before; they're bumpy but not too bad.

A few miles out of Stebbins, I start to realize that even though the sun is shinning, it's still pretty cold out. Sitting exposed on the speeding sled means that I have a 40-mile-an-hour wind in my face the whole time, my own private wind-chill factor. My feet, sticking out in front of me, go numb; my hands, gripping the sides of the sled, follow suit. My rabbit-fur nose guard is working hard to save my face.

Finally we pull up to the St. Michael store. "Betty needs to get a few things, then we'll take her home." They go in while I struggle to get up off the sled and then stagger inside. It's warm and I head for the big heater in the back. Pulling off my gloves with my teeth, I put my stiff, freezing hands an inch from heater's grill. I can't feel a thing.

"Your hands get a little cold back there? You might want to put them in your armpits instead of on the heater. If they get warm too quickly it'll hurt like hell." The words are barely out of Kurt's mouth when I start to feel my hands. The bones are aching inside the flesh. I pull them away from the heater but the pain just keeps growing. "Feels pretty bad, doesn't it? It won't last too long."

Why the hell didn't he mention the armpit trick *before* I cooked my fingers on the heater? I tell Kurt I'll walk home. It feels like I've got miniature mob enforcers inside each of my fingers, working them over from the bone out; a slightly bigger goon is pummeling my palm. The Mafiosi don't let up on my hands for hours and my toes don't thaw for days.

CHAPTER THIRTY-FIVE

ESKIMO OLYMPICS

THE KIDS ARE AT SCHOOL early, especially for a Monday morning. They're excited because St. Michael is hosting an Eskimo-Indian Olympics this weekend. Everyone is practicing their seal hops, ear pulls and high kicks for the games and their Eskimo dancing and rapid-fire Beluga *muktuk* chewing for the cultural competitions. Even kids who aren't competing are in the gym by 7 am. Circus is all but forgotten.

After a frustrating day, I get home to find Kurt making sushi with Spam, what he calls "Spam musubi" — a mound of flavored rice topped with green flecks ("secret family recipe") covered by a slider-sized slab of Spam broiled in a secret sauce ("if I tell you what's in it, I'll have to kill you"), all wrapped in an *obi* of dried seaweed.

"My wife grew up in Hawai'i — you can imagine how much she hated the cold out here — so we always ate Hawaiian food in the winter. She just sent me a care package of sushi rice, dried seaweed and secret ingredients. I brought a few tins of Spam home from the cafeteria, slipped a slack-key guitar CD into the stereo and, violà, we're on the islands." The musubi is surprisingly tasty and the music is great; unfortunately, I'm not in a mood to enjoy Hawaii-on-the-Tundra.

"We didn't get anything done today and I'm afraid I'm going to lose a whole week of teaching. I love watching the kids practice for the Olympics but I'm not being paid to be a sports fan."

"Yeah, you're right; the kids are pretty jazzed about the meet. We got five other villages coming in — lots of old friends, maybe some new kids to play with or flirt with or . . . a little more than flirting." Kurt winks and

I see a glimpse of who he might have been in high school. "And there are prizes and food. Pretty exciting." Principal Kurt is back.

We sit for a while, sipping our smuggled bottles of Primo, Hawai'i's Original Beer. We finish the sushi and Kurt gets up to clear the plates, "I tried some of the games when I was in Unalakleet, thought I might be good because I played ball in college. Man, that stuff is hard and I didn't even try the painful ones like the ear pull — no way I'm looping a leather strap around my ear and letting another guy try to pull it off with his ear. But the one-legged jump looked good. You saw them practicing? Stand on one leg, jump up and kick a little dingus hanging from a basketball hoop and land back on that same leg. I could get three feet, maybe 40 inches. Sounds pretty good, right? We've got 9-year-olds who can beat that. Most of the competitors do five and a half or six feet; champions get up to seven feet. Amazing."

He hands me another beer and asks, "You try anything today? I'll bet you'd be good at 'em; a lot of the stuff looks like circus moves, all that balance and strength." I had tried a few games after school — the seal hop (racing across the floor on your knuckles in push-up position), the one-leg kick and the two-leg kick. I was absolutely pathetic. I say, "Nay, I didn't try anything. Eskimo Olympics might look like circus but it's not."

Kurt ignores my sour tone, wipes rice off his hands and goes into lecture mode. "Actually, a lot of what they're calling 'Olympics' is stuff Eskimos have been doing for centuries, usually after seal hunts. The young guys, the ones who weren't on the hunt, would show off for the hunting captains, trying to get on the next boat by being the fastest, the strongest, the guy with great balance and a high pain threshold." He starts to take a sip but stops with the bottle a few inches from his lips. "Hey, here's an idea — you could use some of that stuff in your show, kind of an Eskimo Olympics/circus hybrid. You're already using Yup'ik stories, why not add some Yup'ik moves, too? The kids all know the games; just ask them to show you tomorrow."

Kurt's got a good idea but I'm too cranky to admit it. I say I'll think about it, thank him for the little trip to Hawai'i and go off to my room to prep for tomorrow.

THE KIDS LOVE DOING Eskimo Olympics in circus class; even the third graders get excited, although it breaks my heart watching them try to do the jumps and hops and pulls. Nick Wassilie, who is the official St. Michael Eskimo-Indian Olympics coach, abandons his custodian duties to co-teach with me. He's almost too respectful, standing near the door at the beginning of every class until I ask him to coach or show some techniques. Once invited in, he's all in.

Nick likes the idea of mixing traditional Yup'ik skills with circus and the kids love figuring out combo moves — balancing peacock feathers on their noses while seal-hopping across the floor, doing the kicks on stilts, juggling scarves in the blanket toss. By the afternoon, Nick and I are finding ways to use the moves to illustrate stories — the seal hop is obvious but then the two-legged jump, done by a whole class at once, becomes a pod of whales breaching, and a smaller kid doing a one-legged jump into a bigger kid's arms becomes a baby.

By Wednesday night I can start to imagine what the show will look like. Nick wasn't in most of the classes today because he had to get everything ready for the meet, but he set the tone yesterday: Circus is fun and cool and very Eskimo. For the first time here in St. Michael, I feel like we're on a roll, like I'm teaching and learning and growing with this village. In the kitchen, I talk Kurt's ear off while he cooks chicken breasts and I make pasta salad. He listens, making appropriate noises and graciously not saying, "I told you so."

On Thursday, the athletes from other villages descend on St. Michael. The Shaktoolik and Kaltag teams spent last night in Unalakleet, about halfway for both of them. This morning, 40 teenagers and their coaches from the three villages got on snowmobiles and caravanned 70 miles southwest to St. Michael. The weather is perfect, clear and just below zero, so they arrive in time for lunch: meatloaf, mashed potatoes, canned peas and cake for dessert. The kitchen staff is going all out for the visitors, planning an even bigger, better lunch for tomorrow. The gym is electric.

The Stebbins team is supposed to arrive for dinner, a potluck in the gym, but the wind is up by the time school is out. There's speculation that they may not make it tonight. By 6pm, the tables in the gym are full of food, waiting for the Stebbins folks. The other visitors are sitting around, visiting. Kurt has a dozen kids putting out plates and silverware when a gaggle of fifth graders barges into the gym, screaming, "They're coming!"

FRIDAY'S LUNCH IS A FEAST: scrambled eggs with salmon, French toast, PBJs, canned corn and huge bowls of *akutaq*. The gym is so crowded kids have to sit on each other's laps to eat. I imagine this same scene in a San Francisco school: cursing, fights, suspensions and possibly lawsuits. I eat at the teachers' table, happy for a little room and sad that I may never be as happy as these kids are, crammed together on cafeteria benches eating *akutaq*.

The talk among the teachers is about the final team, seven athletes and their coach flying in from Little Diomede Island. Little Diomede is just on the U.S. side of the International Date Line; Big Diomede is two and a half miles away on the Russian side, a day ahead of its American neighbor. They are the definition of remote. This is the first time Little Diomede has fielded an Eskimo-Indian Olympic team and they were planning to make the three-hour flight by charter this morning. Even though the storm has passed, we haven't heard their plane.

Lunch is over and my seventh-grade class has a few extra students, athletes from the other villages. I don't even try to teach; Nick runs a training session while I stand back and admire the height of their jumps and how long they can have their ears pulled without losing a lobe. As I'm walking to my next class, I hear a plane and then dodge students racing out to the runway. The Little Diomede team has arrived and school's out for the weekend.

Friday night features lots of Eskimo dancing, a *muktuk* eating contest and the Blanket Toss, which is just what it sounds like, only the blanket is a walrus skin. The athletes almost touch the ceiling of the gym before flipping or running in place or even dancing on their way down.

By the time I say "good-night" to Kurt I'm hoarse from screaming. He is too.

THE GYM IS PACKED AGAIN by 9 am. Saturday for the Indian Stick Pull, Two-Foot High Kick, Ear Pull Finals and something called Drop the Bomb, which I somehow miss. Before lunch, we watch the Native Regalia Contest: old women in stunning fur *kusbuks* and fur hats that stick up like crowns; young women in vibrant gingham *kusbuks* and lots of beads — headbands, earrings, pendants and beaded boots; 3-year-olds wearing impossibly cute little winter *kusbuks* with mittens on brightly braided strings around their necks and fur ruffs that are three times the diameter of their faces.

I slip back to the house for lunch and a break from the crowd while Kurt sticks around for an afternoon of leftovers and visiting. In the midst of all the cuteness and sweat and straining sinews, there is something deeply painful going on with the group from Little Diomede: a brother and sister on the team are half African-American (I don't know the backstory), and the other kids call them "niggermos." It sounded like a Yup'ik word until I realized it was a horribly racist English portmanteau. The sister, who is about 13, sticks close to her younger brother and no one sticks close to them — they eat alone in the crowded gym and sit in the bleachers with a few feet of empty space on all sides. I keep thinking of stories of how "Amerasian" kids were treated in Vietnam after the war.

The Girls Seal Hop is the first competition of the evening; the 13-year-old sister is representing Diomede. Six girls line up on the hardwood floor in push-up position with their hands in fists. When Nick Wassilie says "Go!" they start hopping across the gym on their toes and knuckles, legs and arms straight. They all go back and forth twice before one girl's arms buckle and she collapses face-down on the floor. The other athletes keep going; the girl lies there for a few seconds before getting up and walking to her seat to a round of mild applause. As they turn to start another lap, a second girl goes down and, a moment later, the home team girl's right arm slips off to the side and she falls on her face. There is an audible gasp and when she gets up there's a streak of blood on the floor. The crowd is still cheering for her when the Stebbins kid stops and slowly droops to the floor, spent.

Now it is down the Diomede girl and one other. They go another length of the gym, just the two of them, evenly matched. As they turn the corner into their fourth lap, the other girl slips and falls. The girl from Little Diomede stops, holding her push-up position as the runner-up walks back to her seat. Then the Diomede girl keeps hopping, trailing blood smears behind her. The gym is silent. Every few yards she stops for a moment and then starts hopping again.

There is no reason to keep going — she's won. The game is over. She's the champion, the first Eskimo-Indian Olympics winner from Diomede, ever.

The girl goes another lap and a half. The only sound in the gym is her knuckles hitting the hardwood and her breathing when she rests. Finally she stops and calmly stands up. Her brother runs to her and, hand-in-hand, they slowly walk out of the gym staring straight ahead. No one moves for a long time, until Nick announces the Boys One-Leg Jump and a couple of kids run out to clean the blood off the floor. The athletes take their places and the gym comes back to life.

CHAPTER THIRTY-SIX

TROOPER DAVE AND BROTHER JOE

BY SUNDAY AFTERNOON the teams are gone and on Monday morning the school feels empty. Lots of kids are late or just don't show up, hung-over from the weekend, either metaphorically or literally. Nick has the day off. He deserves it, and I've learned enough to continue working on combo moves with the kids who do show up for class.

Most of the students are in school on Tuesday, and by Wednesday we're back in the groove. Since the kids' show is a week from Friday, we need to get the acts built and rehearsed. I've decided that this show will have a through-line, a loose plot. I want to find a unifying structure that will make the show feel like more than the sum of its parts. A natural cycle can give me what I need: sun-up to sun-down or the turning of the seasons or metamorphosis from caterpillar to butterfly. Thinking about it, I realize that all the shows I've done with kids in Alaska have had a simple cycle: youngest to oldest. That isn't strong enough for this show.

On Wednesday evening I go to the library, a converted shipping crate parked just outside the back door of the school. No one is there but of course the door is unlocked. I turn on the light and see a dozen or so masks hanging on the walls, similar to the ones I saw in Eek on my first trip to the bush. I'd love to play with them but I'm on a different mission. I start to look through the 200 or so books neatly ordered on shelves, trying to find a play that I can simplify and use as a structure for this St. Michael Circus.

There are no plays in the library.

I go to the reference section and find *Bartlett's Familiar Quotations,* the 1957 edition. The Chaucer quotes are in old English, the Bible quotes are too biblical for me and the Mark Twain quotes are too pithy. Luckily, there's a whole section on Shakespeare and in it I find the "Seven Ages of Man" speech from *As You Like It*. Seems promising. I can still go from youngest to oldest, which helps keep the kindergarteners from falling asleep before their act, and the speech gives me some interesting images to work with. I leave a note on the librarian's desk saying that I'm taking the Bartlett's and head back home.

"…the infant, Mewling and puking in the nurse's arms."

Sounds like my kindergarteners. There's a Yup'ik story about a baby who becomes a raven — the K/1 classes can act out the story and balance, or hold, peacock feathers when they become birds. OK, this might work.

I go through the rest of the ages, from the second, "whining schoolboy," to the last, "second childishness," linking them to the stories and tricks we've been working on. I decide to switch number three, the lover "sighing like furnace" with number four, the soldier "sudden and quick in quarrel," since my fifth and sixth graders love to fight and my seventh and eighth graders love to love (or at least talk about love). The last line of the speech, "sans teeth, sans eyes, sans taste, sans everything," seems a bit heavy for high school seniors but I'm willing to give it a try.

THURSDAY IN THE CAFETERIA, I'm eating with Nick and reviewing the details of each class over the noise of a gym full of kids letting off steam. We're figuring out what skills we'll use to illustrate each story, which stories to tell in Yup'ik and how the fourth graders' obsession with Batman fits in the seven ages theme. We're on the sixth age, our wonderfully flamboyant sophomores and juniors doing "the lean and slippered pantaloon with spectacles on nose," when the room suddenly gets quiet. I look up to see two state troopers standing at the door surveying the gym. One of them I recognize from my first day here — he's about my size and age with a shaved head. The other is much younger, small and thin with a dirty blond crew cut under his blue, flat-brimmed Dudley Do-Right hat. He could be a kid dressed as a trooper for Halloween.

The two officers see us, the older one nods and they walk to our table.

Everyone in the room watches them in silence except Nick, who doesn't look up from his lunch. They stand behind Nick, facing me. The big one says, "Hey Nick, nice to see ya. How's it going? I hear the Olympics went well last weekend. Good on ya."

"Thanks, Dave." Nick looks straight ahead and keeps eating.

"This is Officer Stevenson. He's from Kenai, just transferred up here a couple of months ago."

Nick says, "Nice to meet ya" without turning around and then introduces me. I struggle to get my legs out between the bench and the table, stand up and shake hands. There's an awkward silence as Nick keeps eating. Dave, the big trooper, finally says, "Nick, let's go talk in the office, OK?"

Both troopers turn but Nick sits still.

"We can talk here, Dave. Lunch'll be over in a minute and I've got to get back to work."

Officer Stevenson shifts the holster on his belt but Trooper Dave puts up a hand to stop him. "Nick, let's make this easy. You know why we're here. You know we gotta take you to Anchorage with us. Your lawyer should have you back here at work in a couple of days."

Nick's face is blank, completely neutral. I look around; every kid in the room has the same expression. Only the teachers look shocked; I'm sure I do, too. We're silent for a long time. Then Nick puts his fork down and stands up in one smooth move and looks at me. "Sorry to miss the afternoon classes." His voice is as relaxed as when we were chatting about the kids. "I like all the Shakespeare stuff — keep it in. I'll see you Monday morning. We'll start rehearsing the acts." He turns and walks past the troopers so suddenly that they have to jog a couple of steps to keep up.

KURT AND I EAT LEFTOVERS for dinner in silence. Neither of us wants to bring up Nick. After I do the dishes, Kurt pours half of the last Primo into a glass and hands me the bottle. We sit back at the table.

"I've known Nick Wassilie since my time in Unalakleet. He's a good man."

"Is he the guy who's accused of molesting a girl?"

"Like I told you that first night, no one believes the girl."

"Someone believes her or they wouldn't have taken Nick to Anchorage."
We sip.

I say, "That high school senior who went to visit her aunt last week —
Charlene? Is she the girl?"

"Can't say. Student confidentiality."

"I'm guessing she is and I'm guessing Charlene's aunt lives in
Anchorage and I'm guessing the troopers have been talking with her
all week."

Kurt's face is blank. I try to put some more pieces together.

"Was Nick molested by that priest back in the '60s?"

Nothing.

"Come on, Kurt, that priest doesn't have confidentiality. Tell me. I'm
in the middle of this as much as you are. I love these kids, too, and Nick
and the rest."

Kurt chugs his beer and puts his glass down hard. "Here's what I
know: About 100 years ago, 60 percent of the folks out here died in
a flu epidemic." Kurt stands up. "The survivors figured their shamans
had lost their mojo, that maybe they even caused the epidemic, and the
Christian missionaries were right there with open arms, ready to save
Yup'ik souls. By the '50s, the Catholic Diocese of Fairbanks was huge,
bigger than the state of Texas, and they were short on priests. A volun-
teer called Brother Joe was sent here in '68 and stayed for seven years."

"Brother Joe. He's the guy?"

"That's what they say, but it's all just rumor."

"What do they say?"

"They say Brother Joe molested every boy in the village."

"Every boy in the village?"

"It's all just gossip. No one knows the real story." Kurt walks to the
door and starts putting on his coat. "All I can say is that Nick is a good
man. Now I need to go see his wife and then find someone to keep my
school clean for the rest of the week. Good night."

CHAPTER THIRTY-SEVEN

THE SEVEN AGES
OF CIRCUS

THE SCHOOL FEELS FLAT on Friday morning, flat like the tundra, flat like the look on Nick's face before he walked out of the cafeteria, flat like my dad on Lithium. No one smiles, no one frowns, no one looks me in the eye. The kids move around like Stepford wives, no hint of emotion. Working on anything creative is impossible. In every class I break out the peacock feathers and scarves — soft, beautiful things that float and flutter.

Kurt is out visiting again on Friday night, trying to bring life back to the village. I just want to curl up and cry. I want to be home, I want to hold my wife and hear her talk about anything but this godforsaken village. How am I going to make it one more week up here, away from her? I'll call her tomorrow but I can't talk about what's really going on since every phone conversation is public, open to anyone who shops in the store, which is everyone.

Kurt's office computer saves me over the weekend. I dig into work, writing letters to would-be *Father-Land* presenters and artistic directors who might commission a new play, updating my writing résumé, then my acting résumé and my directing résumé in case someone wants to put me at the helm of a big production.

I even get going on a project I've been avoiding, a commission I got a month ago to write a musical on the theme of second-hand smoke. Second-hand smoke? That's like asking a painter to do a portrait of beige. But it was a commission for a play so I should have been excited. I dutifully interviewed a pulmonologist before I flew to Alaska and I haven't thought about it since.

Rereading my interview with the doctor, I get the idea of making it a *Fantastic Voyage*-type story, shrinking the protagonists down to microscopic size and sending them into someone's lungs. The protagonists could be superheroes; I come up with the names Lungman and Windpipe. I need a villain, of course, and go for the obvious — The Smoke Genie — and give him two obvious minions, Tar and Nicotine. Before dinner on Sunday, I've got a title — *Lungman and Windpipe's Excellent Adventure* — a few rough scenes and a stanza of lyrics to give to the composer when I get home:

> You breathe air in through your nose and mouth,
> It goes down your windpipe and then heads south,
> Down t' the air sacs or alveoli,
> Which live right next door to a capillary.
> Veins and lungs make a deal, win/win,
> They trade carbon dioxide for oxygen.

Best of all, I haven't obsessed about Nick or the girl, Charlene, who are now off in Anchorage, or Brother Joe or the third graders or even the show I have to piece together before I fly home.

MONDAY MORNING AND NICK isn't at school. At lunch, Kurt tells me he won't be back until at least Thursday. I want to ask more but the look on Kurt's face stops me. Nick's not coming back any time soon.

Over the week, I build the show with the help of the teachers, using Shakespeare's seven ages as a structure with some Yup'ik stories and some stories the kids made up. The fifth and sixth graders, my soldiers "sudden and quick in quarrel," are doing *Batman vs. the State Troopers,* using a lot of the Eskimo Olympic/circus combo moves. Some of them won prizes for their Eskimo dancing so we've added that to the mix.

Kurt visits my classes when he can, cheering for the kids' routines. The school is not back to normal but the excitement of a show pulls most of the students out of their funk. No one talks about Nick or Charlene, including Kurt. "Student and employee confidentiality."

Thursday morning I come in to find posters of clown faces, painted by the kids, all over the gym walls: A Bozo look-alike with a single daisy sprouting from his head; a tramp clown with stubble and x'ed-out eyes; an accidentally abstract brown face with white hair, a blue nose and lines on its chin that are common in Yup'ik masks. One poster just says "CIRC" in big letters and then a tiny "us" inside the mouth of the final C. CIRC-us.

It's the last period of the day and the high school seniors have a couple of surprises for me. First, Charlene is back from Anchorage. She's a tall, shy girl with newly permed shoulder-length black hair and hard eyes. The other kids treat her carefully, as if she might crumble or lash out at any moment. The second surprise is a new story that the class has decided to tell instead of the Old Timers' Acrobatic Act we've been working on: "second childishness...sans teeth, sans eyes, sans taste, sans everything (except cartwheels)."

The act they want to do is about the trickster Raven and how the world went from darkness to light. They've been getting stories from elders in the village and, they tell me, most the old folks agreed that this one is OK to perform. I start to argue for our well-rehearsed acrobatic act, but when I see their faces go blank, I know it is Raven or nothing.

"Have you decided who is playing which role?"

Nine sets of eyebrows shoot up and they start talking over each other, telling me the story and explaining how they'll do the northern lights with scarf juggling and make the old man's house with an acrobatic pyramid. They tell me who is playing Raven, who is the old man — "See, we're still doing an old man for your Shakespeare thing" — and who is the old man's daughter who gets impregnated by Raven. It's Charlene.

They stop and look at me. Do I understand what they're doing? Will I let them use this circus act to talk about the pain in their village? Will I treat them like kids or let them take a giant step into the world of adulthood, of stories and metaphors, images and village politics?

I say, "Let's see the Raven story" and sit down as they rehearse for the next 40 minutes; intense and oblivious to me.

FRIDAY MORNING I TRAIN the teachers and some parent volunteers how to put on makeup. Kurt has cancelled classes, giving us the day to get ready for the afternoon show. At lunch, the entire fourth grade, all 13 of them, is sitting in a row with their full-white clown faces. They are very cute and I pray they still look good at showtime, three hours from now. Their teacher, a small, quiet Eskimo woman in her mid-twenties, has her own makeup on: big green half-circles above her eyes and a green oblong that extends from her nose to her cheeks to her chin, with yellow dots on the green. As the little clowns watch and giggle, their teacher gets on all fours and hops around the table saying, "I'm a frog! I'm a frog! I'm a frog!"

After lunch, I take the ninth graders into the library so they can get ready away from the rest of the school. They've had a tough time of it, partly because they're 13 years old and partly because I got too attached to my "seven ages of man" structure, saddling them with age five, The Justice...

> ...In fair round belly with good capon lined,
> With eyes severe and beard of formal cut,
> Full of wise saws and modern instances...

This means nothing to these kids.

My new idea is to get them into Yup'ik mask makeup and dressed in traditional clothes borrowed from grandparents, great aunts and great uncles. Looking like this, a simple parade on stilts to the beat of Eskimo drums — a few men have offered to play — will give us a strong Yup'ik feel at the all-important moment about two-thirds of the way through the show. Beards, capons and wise saws will have to wait for another time.

Getting them to sit still while I carefully re-create the masks on their faces is another story. After nearly an hour, I've only got one girl done in a starker version of the half black/half white motif; her right profile is pure white with only a few black lines and her left is a negative image. The other kids have washed off the few lines they let me paint or avoided getting any makeup on at all. With only 45 minutes until showtime, I have to go set up the gym and work on converting the younger kids' pre-show nerves into performance energy.

I leave the makeup, tell the ninth graders to get ready on their own and walk back to the gym. I'm pretty sure we'll have a drum solo instead of a stilt parade but I can't do anything about it now.

CHAPTER THIRTY-EIGHT

RAVEN AND THE SUN AND THE MOON AND THE STARS

IT'S CIRCUS TIME in St. Michael.

The K/1 cuties become baby ravens.

The little second graders and the addled third graders are led by the white-faced fourth graders, makeup only slightly smeared, in a wonderfully whiny schoolboy act, "creeping like snails (and seals and whales and foxes) unwillingly to school."

Batman vs. the State Troopers is one long chase with Batman riding dogsleds, boats and Cessnas (made of other children) while the clumsy state troopers try to escape on horseback (stilts used like hobby horses).

The middle schoolers woo each other on rolla bollas, giving bouquets of peacock feathers and putting juggling scarves over their faces as veils when they finally marry.

Now it's the ninth graders' turn. They're not here.

The drummers play and chant. We wait for a few moments and then the side door of the gym opens, letting in a gust of frigid air. The girl with the half-and-half makeup walks onto the stage dressed in an ornate fur *kusbuk* and beautiful boots. The rest of the class follows in a straight line, each face a Yup'ik mask and each body dressed in clothes two generations old. They walk calmly across the hardwood to the pile of stilts. Each kid picks up a pair and then walks back onto the stage two feet taller. The drummers change rhythm to match their steps. They parade back and forth and when the last boy steps off his stilts, the audience erupts. The clapping gets faster, the drums start again and the kids get back on their stilts to parade around the stage a few more times.

When the music finally stops, the sophomores and juniors tumble on, a troupe of "slippered pantaloons" — old farts in oversized PJs and mop-head wigs. Their clown act includes everything from classic slapstick, with wigs flying everywhere, to geriatric Eskimo Olympics. The audience is howling and the kids keep going, improvising new shtick until I finally step onstage to introduce the last act.

"Ladies and Gentleman, teachers and students, elders and babies, welcome to our final act. You have seen the infants, the whining schoolboys, the fighters, the lovers, the stilt parade of Yup'ik tradition and the old clowns of the tundra. Now I call your attention to the senior class, the young men and women who are the future of St. Michael, as they present their own interpretation of *Raven and the Sun and the Moon and the Stars.*"

<u>Storyteller</u>
Long, long ago there was no sun, no moon and no stars. The only light came from the Ghosts of Dead Children dancing in the sky, what we now call the Northern Lights.

Three smaller kids stand on three bigger kids' shoulders; the top acrobats drop lots of red, pink and blue scarves

In the darkness, the Ghosts of Dead Children would sweep living children away to the underworld. Eskimo families huddled in their huts, scared and crying for light.
Raven heard their cries and took pity on them.

Raven enters from the audience

<u>Raven</u>
I will find some light to put in the sky.

Drummers play; Raven does a flying dance

Look, a light in that window.

<u>Storyteller</u>
The window was in the wall of a small house and in the house sat an Old Man.

Six acrobats make three walls of a house; Old Man enters and sits on a kneeling actor

Hanging on the walls like big balloons were three seal bladders.

Three actors enter, holding inflated opaque garbage bags with flashlights in them

One bladder held the sun, another held the moon, and stars floated in the third seal bladder. As Raven was looking through the window, the Old Man's Daughter came out of the house for water.

Charlene enters, holding a traditional woven basket

<u>Raven</u>
Quick. I will turn myself into a berry leaf and float on the water she is drinking.

Charlene drinks from the basket

<u>Storyteller</u>
Once inside of the Daughter, Raven grew to look like a human boy, a baby.

Raven goes between Charlene's legs and stands up under Charlene's kusbuk

The girl was scared.

Charlene

How did this happen to me?

Charlene cries as she gives birth to Raven, who crawls away

Charlene exits; Old Man and Raven act out the following narration

Storyteller

One day, when his mother was out, Baby Boy Raven began to scream and reach for the bladder balloons. To make him stop, the Old Man gave him the one that held the stars inside of it. Raven popped the balloon and the stars flew up the chimney, bringing light to the sky.

Lights out in gym; flashlights play on walls and ceiling

The next day, Baby Boy Raven again began to cry as he reached for the balloons, so the Old Man gave him the moon, which Raven released into the sky as well.

Lights up as Charlene enters

Charlene

Father, Father, come look at the shining moon and the twinkling stars!

Storyteller

But the Old Man was angry that he had to share the moonlight and starlight.

All three act out the following narration

The third time Baby Boy Raven cried, the Old Man pretended not to hear. The baby cried louder and louder for a whole day and night until it was too much for his Daughter.

Charlene
Father, please give my baby the last balloon.

Storyteller
The Old Man put the balloon inside a walrus hide and sewed it up. The baby tried and tried to free the sun but he could not. At last he turned back into Raven and ripped open the walrus skin with his sharp beak. Then he flew out the door with the sun, up into the sky, laughing up a storm. The Old Man stood in the sunlight, raging, but his daughter was overjoyed.

Charlene
People, people! You asked for light; the light is here!

Storyteller
Eskimo families came out and danced in the light of the sun.

Drummers begin; Charlene leads an Eskimo dance

Storyteller
That night, when the sun went down, the Ghosts of Dead Children came.

Lights out in gym; cast members juggle scarves while actors shine flashlights

But they could not take any more Eskimo children to the underworld because the light of the sun and the moon and the stars cut through the darkness.

Lights on for final bow

CODA

Venice Beach, California
Fall 2007

I'M SITTING ON A BALCONY overlooking Venice Beach, wearing swimming trunks and down booties. It's been a decade since I froze my toes in St. Michael but they still give me trouble, even in the SoCal heat. I'm on tour with Cirque du Soleil and we're here in L.A. for a long run. My wife and kids just left for home, driving home up the 101. Seeing my family every week is so sweet after months of Skype calls from hotel rooms thousands of miles away. Knowing that I'll be off tour and home for good in another month is even sweeter.

For the five years before joining Cirque du Soleil, I was home writing a string of commissions — adaptations of *Oedipus Rex* and the Book of Esther, a circus *Monkey King* and a musical version of *Alice in Wonderland*. After years of struggling to become a playwright, I had finally made it and then pretty quickly got tired of writing all the time. I missed audiences, I missed moving my body, I missed the community of a cast. I even missed feeling uncomfortable in strange new worlds.

Touring with Cirque du Soleil is different than my trips to Alaska and Nebraska: We're a traveling town, a circus town, smaller than even the tiniest Eskimo village with a United Nations worth of cultures. We pitch our tent in one city after another, living in a bubble separate from the world we travel through. In Atlanta, Denver, Tokyo and L.A., audiences come to our tent. They watch us but we can't see them, we don't hear their stories. They go home and we take the shuttle back to the hotel. On the tundra and in the Heartland, I was right in the middle of their towns, their problems, their history. Now I'm traveling with my people in my circus world, even though I don't understand most of the conversations backstage.

Every day, when I arrive at the tent, I try to greet to everyone in the right language. For some folks who are particularly proud of their English skills, it means "good morning" or even "what's up?" For others it is *bonjour* or *ohayō gozaimasu*. I can get a few more sentences in a few languages but after that we either switch to English or say good-bye. For all my traveling, I am still very much an American, a *gussak,* trying to connect with people from far-flung worlds and, as often as not, coming up short. There are still borders to cross.

But for the next 24 hours I get to be in a smaller bubble, my bubble. Tomorrow is our day off. The sun is setting over the Pacific, pelicans are diving in formation and the Sunday crossword is on the little glass-topped table beside me. Tonight, life is simple.

I go into the kitchenette to get a pen and pour myself a shot of single malt, the final touch. The front section of the paper is open on the counter and I notice a picture of a snow-covered village. The caption says the town is St. Michael, Alaska.

> "Addressing one of the darkest chapters of sexual abuse in its history, the Roman Catholic Church has agreed to pay $50 million in damages to Eskimo victims and their families."

My god, 50 million dollars. That's a lot of damage. I think about Brother Joe and Nick Wassilie.

> "The alleged victims, now in their 40s and 50s, kept quiet until last year when they saw stories about the Catholic sexual abuse scandal on their television sets nightly. After strong encouragement from their adult children, 28 men from St. Michael and neighboring Stebbins finally broke their silence."

I think about Charlene and the Raven who are now adults in a village with more money and fewer secrets; fewer secrets, at least, about Brother

Joe. And I think about the gasoline-sniffing third graders, who would have been last year's graduating class — if any of them graduated.

> "Many folks say that Joseph (Brother Joe) Lundowski gave them their first drinks. They say Brother Joe had a 'monkey room' where he doled out candy, juice and food, along with holy wine and homebrew. Adjacent to the monkey room was a bedroom.
> "'We couldn't tell anyone before because no one would believe us,' said retired school custodian Nick Wassilie, 'We are happy for this settlement but it is too late for our people who have died or killed themselves.'"

The Ghosts of Dead Children, the Aurora Borealis.

> "'Brother Joe had power in the villages,' said a lawyer for the Eskimo victims. 'He had language power. He had political power. He had racial power. He had the power to send you to hell.'"

Not any more. Sometimes things change. I want to go back to St. Michael to teach Charlene's kids to juggle. I want to eat spam and paint Eskimo masks on kids' faces. I want to write a play about breaking the silence, or help Charlene write a play for the whole village, telling even more secrets.

But they might not need me now. Dougie and Barnsie might already be there, making a show with every kid in the village. Some of Paul Paul's students might have grown up to be teachers, showing off Yup'ik masks and sharing the old stories. Charlene might be the new St. Michael school custodian.

I leave my Scotch on the table and go back out on the balcony. It's twilight. There's a warm breeze coming off the ocean.

The End

GRATITUDE

WRITING THIS BOOK was as much an adventure as the story it tells. To give thanks to everyone who contributed, I would have to take a grand gratitude tour, which might start by boarding a metaphoric plane. I would sit next to my wife, Sherry Sherman, and our boys Micah Sherman-Raz and Joshua Sherman-Raz. In the rows around us would be the folks who read various drafts of *The Snow Clown*, including Sherry, Jael Weismen (who also co-wrote and directed the play *Father-Land*), Zofia Burr, David Carlyon, Chris Ertel and Natasha Kalusa. My editor, Douglas Cruickshank, would be sitting with my copy editor Erfert Fenton and book designer Tracy Cox.

Landing in Alaska, I'd thank Janet Goulston, Wendy Parkman, Francis Evans, Mark Sackett, Craig Sjogerman and all the other San Francisco artists who toured the tundra in the '80s and '90s. We'd go thank the Alaska Arts Council folks who got us out into the bush and then safely home. A series of short hops in small planes would allow me to thank the people who live in villages on the Yukon/Kuskukwim Delta, from Bethel to Eek, Kwethluk to St. Michael. Before leaving Alaska, I'd have to stop in Fairbanks to thank Patty Duval, the rest of Dr. Ogstad's Traveling Medicine Show and the other musicians, rodeo riders and artists who welcomed me into the world of the Alaska State Fair and then into their homes.

The next stop would be Lincoln, Nebraska, where I'd go right to The Mill to get a cup of coffee and thank my aunt Hilda Raz and uncle Dale Nordyke. Then I'd hug Ron Bowlin, Kit Voorhees, David Bagby and all the other people who made the Artist Diversity Residency Program a unique and powerful program. Before I got back on the plane, I'd thank all the students I performed for and wrote plays with and the teachers who shared their classrooms with me.

Landing back in the Bay Area, I'd have to shout out a huge "thank you" to all the circus performers, dancers, musicians and theater folks who make up the vibrant community that has been my artistic family for more than four decades. I hope we can always throw cartwheels on the borders between us.

ABOUT THE AUTHOR

Jeff Raz has performed nationally and internationally for decades, starring in circuses (Cirque du Soleil, Pickle Family Circus and more) and plays, including Shakespeare's *Comedy of Errors* on Broadway. He is a graduate of Dell'Arte International, has written 15 plays, including *Father-Land* with Jael Weisman, and has directed dozens of circus, puppet and theater productions. He cofounded Vaudeville Nouveau in 1982, the S.F. New Vaudeville Festival in 1985, The New Pickle Family Circus in 1993, The Clown Conservatory in 2000 and the Medical Clown Project in 2010. His first book, *The Secret Life of Clowns: A backstage tour of Cirque du Soleil and The Clown Conservatory,* was launched at the Smithsonian in 2017. Jeff continues to write, perform, direct, and teach as well as work globally as a communications consultant with Stand & Deliver. He lives in Alameda, California, with his wife, Sherry Sherman, and their sons Micah and Joshua.

ALSO BY JEFF RAZ

Fiction
The Secret Life of Clowns: A backstage tour of Cirque du Soleil and The Clown Conservatory

Plays
Father-Land (with Jael Weisman)
Lungman and Windpipe's Excellent Adventure (music by Johannes Mager)
Noah's Floating House Party (with students at UNL)
All Tangled Up (with students at UNL)
The Whole Megillah, Abridged
Oedipus the King
The Road to Hades (music by Johannes Mager)
Wonderland (music by Johannes Mager)
Monkey King: A Circus Adventure (music by Johannes Mager)
The Great Big Rainbow Tent (music by Johannes Mager)
The Wedding of Sir Gawain and Dame Ragnelle (music by Shira Kammen)
Birth Mark (with Jael Weisman)
Dog Tails (music by Mark Izu)
Return of the Sun
Appetite for Books